Resource
Management

Edited by
TONY BOWERS

CROOM HELM
London • New York • Sydney

© 1987 Tony Bowers
Croom Helm Ltd, Provident House, Burrell Row,
Beckenham, Kent, BR3 1AT
Croom Helm Australia, 44-50 Waterloo Road,
North Ryde, 2113, New South Wales

Published in the USA by
Croom Helm
in association with Methuen, Inc.
29 West 35th Street
New York, NY 10001

British Library Cataloguing in Publication Data

Special educational needs and human
    resource management.
    1. Exceptional children — Education
    2. School personnel management
    I. Bowers, Tony
    371.9′042   LC3965
    ISBN 0-7099-5014-4

Library of Congress Cataloging-in-Publication Data

Special educational needs and human resource management.

    Bibliography: p.
    Includes index.
    1. Teachers of handicapped children—In-service
training. 2. Handicapped children—Education.
3. Mainstreaming in education. I. Bowers, Tony.
LC4019.8.S66 1987   371.9   87-3606
ISBN 0-7099-5014-4

Printed and bound in Great Britain by Mackays of Chatham Ltd, Kent

CONTENTS

Acknowledgements

List of Figures

Introduction   1

1. Human Resources and Special Needs:
    Some Key Issues   4
        Tony Bowers

2. National Initiatives in Special Education
    Training: Intention and Impact   27
        Ivor Ambrose

3. Approaches to Staff Development   43
        Alvin Jeffs

4. Mainstream Support Work - What is it all about?   66
        Maggie Balshaw

5. Internal and External Support:
    Roles and Definitions   82
        Tony Bowers

6. Bringing the Special Needs Department
    out of the Cupboard   99
        Martyn Rouse

7. Students with Special Needs in Further Education   111
        Alastair Kent

8. What's the Job About?   123
        Sue Knight, Rosalie White,
        Barbara Tyler and Brian Steedman

9. Investing in Successful Parental Partnership   136
        Allan Sigston

10. Involving Pupils in their own Assessment   149
        Irvine Gersch

References   171

Index   182

ACKNOWLEDGEMENTS

My thanks go to all the contributors to this book for taking on this burden in addition to their jobs. They go also to the Administration of the Cambridge Institute of Education for making facilities available for its preparation. Finally, I would like to express my gratitude to Jean Jarvis for her unstinting efforts in preparing the manuscript and steering the book to completion.

Tony Bowers

FIGURES

Figure   I: The Backdrop to a S.E.N. Staff
               Development Policy   46

Figure   II: An Appraisal of Peter's Performance
               by a Head with whom Peter worked   48

Figure III: The Programme for Action   49

Figure   IV: Peter's Preferred Methods of
               In-service Development   50

Figure   V: Peter's Plan of Action   52

Figure   VI: Staff Development Programme
               on larger scale   54

Figure VII: Continuum indicating the Degree
               of Pupil Involvement   167

INTRODUCTION

by Tony Bowers

At one time, the obvious career route for a teacher
whose main interest lay in working with handicapped or
learning-disabled pupils would lead him or her into a special
school. Not only did such schools tend to be more favourably
blessed with appropriate educational equipment and learning
aids, and to have a concentration of staff with common
interests and concerns; they were likely also to provide a
clearly-defined route for eventual professional advancement
and usually, through a policy of encouraging extended
training, would give their staff the opportunity to obtain
further relevant qualifications. Times, though, are changing.

Three separate yet interconnected developments make it
no longer such a simple issue. Firstly, over the last ten
years there has been an increasing recognition that learning
problems of one kind and another, whether the result of
factors within the child or his or her environment, or simply
the product of bad or inappropriate teaching, occur with
considerable frequency in ordinary schools. As a result, such
schools have created and developed specialist posts for
teachers of children with special educational needs; more
crucially, though, the idea of "whole-school" responsibility
for pupils with learning difficulties has evolved, causing
those specialists to have to re-evaluate their previously
largely child-centred and child-involved roles. Coupled with
this, we have seen an acknowledgement that many children with
more moderate learning difficulties, who previously had been
consigned to special schools for the remainder of their
education, can reasonably be expected to cope with mainstream
provision as long as some appropriate specialist support is
given to them or to their teachers. The populations of
special schools are therefore likely in some cases to
contract, or to change, or to be subject to a considerably
greater degree of flux than was previously the case.
Finally, the whole nature of in-service education and staff
development is under review. No longer is the one-year

1

institution-based course, or its equivalent, assumed to be the most appropriate vehicle for developing skills and knowledge which will be of direct relevance to the school and ultimately the child. As a result, we are likely to see less emphasis on obtaining formal qualifications for in-service education, with far greater attention being paid to devising training which will have a direct impact on teachers' behaviour and, through this, on schools.

Changing views have led to changing - or changed - jobs. A glance at the relevant sections of the 'situations vacant' pages in educational journals reveals job titles and duty descriptions which in many cases would have been difficult or impossible to find just five years ago. It is evident that these call for ways of working and for associated people-orientated management skills which have not traditionally been expected of teachers in special education. Additionally, there is a growing acknowledgement that teachers themselves are only one of the groups of people who influence and have a stake in the development of a child. They constitute an important set of what we may term "human resources" and are, of course, organised and paid for this purpose. Many others, though, also form available resources, not least among them parents and the children themselves.

It would be possible for a book concerned with human resource development to concentrate on what have come to be called "multiprofessional issues": looking at the ways in which differing professionals conceptualise their roles in relation to children with special needs, and at methods of their working as members of that frequently heard word a "team". This book is intended primarily for educators, however, and its thrust has been directed principally towards educational institutions and those who work in or from them. While the interface of educational and other professions is at times considered, the key issues addressed relate to ways in which those already existing resources, namely teachers in ordinary schools, parents and the children themselves, can best be mobilised and utilised. At times, differing views may be presented. Such apparent contradictions are no bad thing, since they highlight the fact that there are no "right" or "wrong" answers in using people as resources, only shades of appropriateness which depend on a variety of situational and personal circumstances.

The first parts of this book look at general management issues in relation to special needs teaching staff in their roles within more integrated settings, followed by some broad and then more specific issues in staff development for such work. Later chapters look at the idea of support and the active provision of this. Special educational provision beyond the age of sixteen, and the resource consequences of this are then reviewed, while final sections look at some of the ways in which parents and children can be mobilised as

resources both in decision-making and in programme implementation.

This book does not focus on special schools, although
some of the authors look at ways of redeploying the expertise
and experience which may lie in these; indeed, one of the
four contributors who attempt to bring their own jobs to life
in the pages of Chapter 8 works in such a school. The main
concerns of this book do not lie in whether special or
mainstream schools are "better" for pupils with special
needs, however, but with considering ways in which that most
fickle, unpredictable, yet versatile and potentially most
effective resource, the person, can best be encouraged and
deployed in special education today.

Chapter One

HUMAN RESOURCES AND SPECIAL NEEDS: SOME KEY ISSUES

Tony Bowers

Introduction

It is quite obvious to anyone working in education that the pressure for change and to change has been enormous in the last few years. This is no less so in special education. At one time, this branch of the education service offered a backwater which was relatively untroubled by such traumas as comprehensivisation, the raising of the school-leaving age or curricular reform. Special education was seen largely as occurring in special schools and units, and these, whilst possibly responsive to changes in the wider system, were not called upon fundamentally to reappraise their role definitions and working practices. This is no longer so; the past few years have seen considerable pressure for reform of the ways in which local education authorities conceptualise and attempt to meet special educational needs.

It is not the purpose or intention of this chapter to chronicle the nature of these changes or the motivating forces behind them. Any state of ambiguity in a system is likely to lead to a scramble for influence. This is true of an unstable nation state and equally true of special educational provision. Competing perspectives can be found in the burgeoning literature in the field. The general view is perhaps well summarised by Mittler (1986) in a preface to a book concerned with severe learning difficulties, in which he envisages significantly increased responsibility being placed upon mainstream schools for the education of children with severe and even profound learning handicaps. At the same time, as I point out in a later chapter, with the prevailing view among educationalists that a child's failure to adapt to the expectations of a school is in fact a failure of the school itself in determining its provision, we have seen a movement towards a "whole school" approach in mainstream schools. Martyn Rouse discusses this further in Chapter 6; what it means, though, is that with an attempt to involve all teaching staff in meeting special educational needs, the specialist has to be more than a good teacher with particular knowledge in areas of assessment and intervention. He or she has now to be also an advocate, an adviser, a shaper of attitudes.

New jobs for old

Looking at the ways in which special schools might change their roles in response to the 1981 Education Act, Dessent (1984) considers just how and to whom resources might be delivered. He discusses transportable material resources but also looks at the human resource implications of the altered roles of staff. As he points out, the very nature of the job which has attracted many staff to work in such schools is likely radically to change. For someone whose interests lie in working with individual children, directly assisting their development, relating to them and perhaps to their parents, it can come as a major shock to give time and energy to pupils they may seldom see and who are the responsibility of another teacher, professional or parent.

A failure to recognise that people enter professions - or subdivisions of those professions - and choose to develop their subsequent careers in ways that give them satisfaction, can lead to major management problems. I was recently involved in looking at a service for hearing-impaired pupils in one L.E.A. The school for the deaf had been closed and staff members had become part of an area support team. However, this membership was largely an administrative one, because each of them was placed separately in a local mainstream school which had been designated as an area resource school for hearing-impaired pupils. Because integration was the keynote of this change, pupils with the special needs associated with deafness were placed in ordinary classes throughout each school. As a gesture of support for these schools, the teachers of the deaf became extra members of staff who taught a normal timetable; in a primary school, this meant becoming a class teacher, while in a secondary school the teacher reverted to the subject specialism for which she initially trained. The purpose was straightforward: each would act as a key person to provide advice on teaching methods to their colleagues who taught hearing-handicapped pupils, and would themselves be integrated as staff members in the schools.

Once a week, the teachers of the deaf - now ordinary class teachers with a resource role - came together for meetings with their area coordinator. What became increasingly evident was the disenchantment of many of them with this new role which had, despite apparent "consultation", been thrust upon them. This manifested itself not in open rebellion but in hostility to the coordinator, in scathing references to the idea of innovation, in complaints over trivial issues in their work and in higher rates of absentee-ism. Additionally, the team coordinator became frustrated at her failure to prevent some members gathering groups of hearing-impaired children together during lunch-times and breaks to work and communicate with them in what she saw as a segregated setting. This was against the whole policy which underlay the new integrated approach.

Further investigation showed that there were a number of issues which had not really been addressed. First, there was the question of a radical change of role and workplace. Many of these teachers of the deaf were not fully committed to what they saw as an imposed decision; despite preliminary consultative meetings, they saw the innovation as already settled upon in response to a prevailing ideology which would have been almost blasphemous to oppose. Even more important, though, was the sense that their present separation from what they saw as "their" pupils had deskilled them. They had trained as ordinary teachers and then taken further qualifi-cations to work in a particular way that they saw as relevant and necessary. Now the message which they were receiving was that they and their training had largely got it wrong. Their surreptitious lunchtime groups were providing them with a way of re-establishing their relevance and identity.

What is the lesson in this? Maybe we have to acknow-ledge that not all change is comfortable, that we can't always expect the same cosy routine that we trained for, and that policies are more important than the niceties of individuals' work preferences. Alternatively, we can look at the poor motivation of these teachers as a management failure: failure to take account of the tendency of all individuals to attempt to meet their needs for self esteem and the recognition of others through their work, failure to prepare them adequately for the changed expectations within their jobs, and failure to provide an adequate support system to deal with the stresses ensuing from the disparity between old and new ways of working. What was evident was that the changed structure was not working in the way in which it was intended to, and that this was a function of the way in which the human, rather than the physical or material, resources were handled.

There is, of course, a tendency for those in education to assume that they are more prone to the exigencies of change than are others members of the public services. This is probably untrue. There have been, and still are, massive changes in the ways in which health and social services workers are organised and in how they view their functions. Some of these parallel many of the actual or envisaged changes in special educational provision. The Warnock Report's (D.E.S., 1978) call for more generic rather than specific courses of training, in fact, reflected an earlier movement of social workers' training and role expectations; until the late 1960s, social workers would be trained for work in particular specialisms such as visual handicap or care of the elderly. Similarly, "integration" has been a theme within social services' child care provision; we have seen the dismantling of many community homes and a strong emphasis on placement in foster care. One aspect of health service provision which is undergoing quite traumatic change in a similar direction is that of mental health. We are seeing the closure or running-down of many psychiatric hospitals, an emphasis on "community care", and a subsequent re-evaluation of the roles of mental health workers such as psychiatric nurses; ways of working for which they were trained are no longer relevant, and new approaches to their patients in entirely different settings are being urged upon them. In many cases, this can lead to demoralisation for staff who feel powerless and deskilled in the face of the change which surrounds them. We can perhaps learn from these examples and from others which parallel many of the developments in services for children with special educational needs.

Two components of success

If you cared to ask most teachers or most educational leaders (head teachers, L.E.A. inspectors, education officers and the like) what their primary aim was, they would probably reply in terms of seeking to provide a high quality of service to their clients, in other words to pupils and therefore to those pupils' parents. However, within those sentiments may lie a variety of methods; it would also be naïve to accept such intentions at face value. Within any organisation, be it school, service or L.E.A., its individual members will seek to meet their own needs. It is likely that the more fundamental security needs will have been met in such individuals, and so we have to look at the varying ways in which, beneath the rhetoric of service provision, individuals seek to maximise their opportunities for recognition, power, influence, social approval, personal revenge, reduced anxiety, heightened arousal, or any of the rewards which go to make for increased satisfaction in working life.

Without these varying individual purposes, usually unspoken and unacknowledged, we might expect to find far more rational and unified organisation of services than in fact exists. We can usefully, therefore, distinguish between expressed values within an organisation - what is said to be important - and core values, or what actually underlies the rhetoric. In a study in the U.S.A., Peters and Waterman (1982) have identified two of the latter which distinguish the best-run organisations from others. These are: (i) a genuine belief on the part of those in leadership positions in the importance of delivering superior quality and service, and (ii) a real regard for the individual rights and requirements of those working in the organisation. What they looked for was more than the payment of hollow lip-service to these ideals; the lesson for special educational services in times of change, when opportunities exist for powerful individuals to maximise their personal needs, is that such values should be central to any strategic plan and to the planning process itself.

All this may sound rather theoretical. It becomes more real when we look at L.E.As in which new services are being built up under the auspices of the Inspectorate or the School Psychological Service which deliberately parallel or compete with services which have been formerly provided by special schools. It is made concrete when we see expertise which has been built up in either mainstream or special schools discounted because it is administratively desirable to establish a demand for new services which have been created or which are planned. It becomes all too apparent when we see staff placed in a position where they can all too easily fail, when asked to take on roles calling for new skills without adequate thought being given to reorientation and effective training.

A fundamental assumption that will be made in this chapter is that people are capable of far more than they often give or are asked to give. Usually this is because they are not provided with the opportunity to do so, the motivation to do so, or both. There are very few pople who set out to be marginal performers at work; in teaching their numbers are probably smaller than in many other walks of life. Yet it would not be difficult in the present climate to identify many people working with pupils with special educational needs whose morale is low and whose energies, both emotional and physical, could be considerably increased in relation to their work. We can explain such phenomena in many terms, but all are reducible to their employing organisations' real lack of commitment to maintaining fully and developing the most complex and potentially effective resource which they possess. People are not like hardware or plant; they are unpredictable, demanding, challenging and temperamental. On the other hand, despite the assumptions of so many managers, they are not subject to planned obsolescence, they do not wear out of their own accord; they have the capacity to grow, to adapt, to mature and to energise the systems in which they operate.

In the remainder of this chapter, I shall address myself to particular issues facing special services providers in ensuring that their effectiveness is not unduly impaired; in particular, issues relating to the growing areas of provision in mainstream schools and in the associated support services will be examined. Until this point much of what has been said has been related particularly to teachers. However, teachers form only one occupational group working with pupils with special educational needs. In a following section, we will look at some of the management considerations which need to be borne in mind in managing groups whose members are drawn from differing disciplines. Before doing this, however, it is perhaps relevant to look at the particular subgroupings of teachers to which this chapter addresses itself.

Categories of special needs teachers

Any attempt to create a typology of teachers working in the education of children with special needs is doomed to be dogged by exceptions and overlap. With the development of "whole school" approaches (see Martyn Rouse's chapter in this book), we have, of course, an attempt to achieve that perfect state where every teacher is committed to, and skilled in, working with children with particular learning or behaviour difficulties. However, that point is generally some distance away, if realistically attainable at all.

This book is primarily concerned with the utilisation of human resources in non-special school settings; many special schools now, though, offer "outreach" work in supporting pupils in ordinary schools whose problems of learning fall within the scope and experience of their staff. In many L.E.A.s we are also seeing the establishment of specialist support services which operate under the aegis of the Special Needs Inspector, Principal Educational Psychologist or Education Officer for Special Education; their precise line of accountability is often dependent on local power relationships and historical precedent. In some cases, such services are "generic", in others they are separated to follow the new, if broader, categories of handicap represented by such terms as "emotionally and behaviourally disturbed", "moderate learning difficulties" or "sensorily impaired". In a few cases, the work of such new services is coordinated with the largely self-developed activities of special schools' outreach staff. More often, unfortunately, they are to some degree in competition with one another in providing overlapping services to client schools or parents at home. This constitutes the second group of teachers, once again providing services to other schools and to their teachers.

It is important to distinguish between this new breed of support teacher, largely directing their energies at other teachers or groups of teachers, and the much longer-established first-line of support. At one time these were termed "peripatetic remedial teachers", their involvement being principally with individual assessment and with devising

9

programmes which they themselves would implement on their visits to schools. Because they had only a limited advisory role and a more direct involvement in intervention, their spread of client schools was usually smaller. I have lapsed into the past tense because in so many L.E.A.s this group of support teachers has become transformed into the former; I go into a more detailed account of their new role requirements in Chapter 5. However, albeit with a more updated job title, this last group still exists in some L.E.A.s. Because of their direct involvement with teaching, in some ways they closely parallel many special school-based outreach teachers.

The fourth group of teachers with whom this chapter is concerned constitute by far~ the largest population. These are the special needs specialists working in ordinary schools. They may be the former "heads of remedial education" and their colleagues whose brief has become widened in the wake of integration and a whole-school orientation to special needs, or the more specialised staff such as the former teachers of the deaf mentioned earlier in this chapter. Or they may be the new special needs coordinators and teachers, products of the one term SENIOS courses mentioned by Ivor Ambrose in his chapter in this book, or of the L.E.A.-inspired training which has begun and will no doubt increase in response to D.E.S. Circular 6/86 (cf. Moore, 1986).

It is now my intention to look at some of the issues and processes which those in leadership positions might bear in mind in any endeavour to develop services involving any of the above roles. Whilst I do not intend to deal at length with the conventional management concerns which are common to most organisations and certainly to all schools, the next section will look briefly at some of these in the context of the appointment and development of special needs teaching staff.

Selection and appraisal

Methods of selection

The model which underlies the selection of teaching staff, and of those given any responsibility for managing others, is one of attempting to predict individual performance. Unless the person has already done the very job for which they apply, this calls for a degree of clairvoyance. It is risky. However, as anyone who has attended a management course will at least be urged to assume, the element of risk can be reduced by adopting systematic procedures: in education these usually involve the gathering of biographical data, the scrutiny of confidential references, the "shortlisting" process and an interview or interviews before final selection occurs. The interview tends to be taken for granted as a primary method of staff selection in education. Depressingly large numbers of those in leadership positions are quite happy with their ability to choose the "best" candidate using such methods almost exclusively, despite Bayne's (1982) state-of-the-art conclusion that "interviewing as currently practised is a poor method of judging people" (p.65).

The type of interview conducted - whether to create a panel of interviewers to see the candidate at once or to set up a series of individual interviews - has been the subject of much discussion. Argyle (1978) treats it as self-evident that panel interviews are less relaxed and generate less useful information than do individual interviews; Bayne (1982) has, though, questioned this assumption, arguing that panel interviews have the virtue of greater efficiency and may, by reducing intimacy, actually be less threatening to some candidates. Although panel interviews are still often favoured in the public services, a recent survey of U.K. commercial organisations (Robertson and Makin, 1986) shows that less than one third favour panel interviews for selection of executives. McHenry (1981), though, has few doubts that a series of individual interviews is preferable for a variety of reasons, but principally because the confident candidate who has "acting" ability is unduly favoured in the panel situation.

Other methods are, of course, frequently used as a back-up to the interview. The most notorious of these is the "confidential" reference, a device with low levels of objectivity, providing little standard for comparison, and probably more suited to maintaining authority in organisations than providing predictive information. Tests may have some utility, though the predictive validity of the traits or abilities which they measure needs to be carefully established in relation to the job in question. My own experience has shown them to be used little if ever in the appointment of teaching staff, although they are used considerably more frequently in management selection (Robertson and Makin, 1986). It is interesting to note that despite a resistance on the part of educational managers to the use of tests measuring personality variables, many still appear willing to make assessments of such traits as flexibility, adaptability, sensibility to others, self-confidence and emotional resilience on the far more tenuous data generated by a selection interview.

I have already mentioned that most selection procedures attempt to predict individual performance. This is fine whilst we expect a job incumbent to act fairly independently of the activities of others; as we have seen, though, special needs posts, with their emphasis on advice and support to other teachers, to parents and to associated agencies, are calling for skills in dealing with other adults and in assisting them in changing behaviours or adapting to new ways of working. As such they involve interactive dependencies, and become more closely akin to a manager's role in most organisations: success will depend on what is accepted as legitimate by significant others around him or her. Predicting behaviour then becomes that much more difficult because it is a function of the person-situation-interaction, or what Bandura (1977) has termed 'reciprocal determinism'.

Any endeavour to select for a given special needs post needs to bear the foregoing in mind, just as attempts to appraise performance do. The traditional selection paradigm, involving the creation of a job description and job specification, may be useful in interviewing, but tends not to embody the concept of person-situation interaction. Assessment centre type exercises (cf. Fletcher, 1982), especially adapted to the kinds of interactive demands which are liable to be placed on the special needs teacher (e.g. Bowers, 1987) are likely to prove more valid in selecting for effective job performance than conventional methods alone. Indeed, Hunter and Hunter (1984) have reported that work-sample tests are among the most valid methods of predicting success in posts involving managerial skills; the crucial point for the selector lies in choosing appropriate work-samples which apply to the dynamic and uncertain task confronting those in special needs support roles.

Any scrutiny of current job descriptions for special needs posts with an element of leadership responsibility will show that at least some - and possibly much - consideration has been given to defining tasks and duties. At one level they appear to set out the requirements of the job and should therefore facilitate selection; at another, many of the phrases we find are potentially useless for two crucial reasons: (i) they have no behavioural anchors (Smith and Kendall, 1963), and (ii) they largely ignore the principle of reciprocal determinism considered above. Phrases such as "ensure that colleagues who teach children with learning difficulties are aware of their special needs", "be prepared to work closely with both primary and secondary teachers", "offer guidance to other departments in the matter of preparing syllabuses to meet the needs of less able children", or "to liaise with teachers and observe within class groups" provide little opportunity for individual selection because they ignore the crucial interaction between the role incumbent and those with whom he or she must work.

One problem is that selectors themselves often know less than they should about the realities of the job; a secondary school head, one deputy, an adviser and a member of the governing body, who might make up the selection team for a comprehensive school special needs coordinator's job, may have no real picture of what actually doing that job entails in terms of time allocation, the particular knowledge and skills required and the power relationships which may be involved. There is a need for considerably more job analysis (e.g. McCormick, 1979) to give an accurate picture of the real requirements of many special needs posts rather than a distanced view of what they ought to entail. At present, most job descriptions of special needs staff are written without any systematic attempt on the part of their line managers to understand and define the realities of the day-to-day elements of the job.

In Chapter 10, Irvine Gersch outlines approaches to using pupils in their own assessment. We might consider applying some of these principles to the job selection process. At present, despite passing lip-service to two-way communication, candidates are in many ways excluded from the decision-making process, presumably on the assumption that they will not reject themselves. However, evidence from the studies of Downs et al (1978) shows that where work-sample tests are used in selection, candidates who perform badly - even when offered the job - tend not to accept it. Appropriate job analysis can lead to the development of such sample tests for use with special educators. They have the advantage of providing candidates with useful information and feedback about their own performance and potential; perhaps the person who has most to lose from a poor decision should be given a more central role in the selection process.

Appraisal

Of the four key systems necessary for ensuring the proper management of any organisation's human resources - selection, appraisal, training and motivation - arguably the second is most important because it is a prerequisite for establishing the other three. Performance appraisal has of late become a key theme in industrial action in teaching and has generated a great deal of fear and anxiety. It has unfortunately become linked to the situation which exists in most organisations where, in a one-to-one setting, a supervisor discusses with a subordinate, areas deserving recognition and areas where improvement is needed. However, if we see performance appraisal in the wider context as any personnel decision that affects the status of employees, we become immediately aware that it has been with us for a very long time. Any confidential reference, any award of a promoted post within a school, any recommendation for secondment to a course of training, must be the product of some appraisal of individual performance; it may be subjective, biased, ill-informed, or all of these, but appraisal will still have taken place.

13

The periodic appraisal model which currently prevails in U.K. educational thinking is actually derived from management by objectives (M.B.O.). M.B.O. developed in the sixties, from a concept said to have originated with Drucker (1954) as a way of rating jobs that are ill-defined and not suited to standard rating schedules. It requires a superior and subordinate to come together and prepare a set of specific and measurable job goals or "objectives". Casteel (1984) has looked at some practical applications of this to special needs teachers. The idea is that the subordinate is then rated on the extent to which the goals set for him or her are attained, together with the quality of goal attainment.

It is not possible or necessarily relevant here to develop a lengthy treatise on the topic of staff appraisal. There are numerous publications which look in detail at its nature, utility and limitations (e.g. Latham and Wexley, 1982). There are, though, a number of points worth noting in relation to the rapidly changing and evolving special needs education field. In 1980, the American Psychological Association (Division of Industrial-Organisational Psychology), after considering methods of staff appraisal, issued the following guidelines:

(i)   Any appraisal method must be based on a systematic examination of the job and the context in which it is performed. This is a crucial point: before appraisal, an appraiser will need to understand how a job is done and what personal characteristics it requires. Summarising the sources of relevant information in achieving this, Howell and Dipboye (1982) suggest that we can look to the individual doing the job to provide us with an account of what it requires, we can look to an outsider seen as an "expert" in doing the job (in education this is likely to be a head of department or an adviser), or we can actually do the job ourselves and record observations on what it is like to do it.

(ii) The job analysis should be conducted at a time when the job is reasonably stable and not in a period of rapid evolution. It needs to be borne in mind that an appraisal based in some part on analysis will not be relevant when things are changing. This applies particularly where the "expert" analysis used so frequently in education, even in an unstructured form, is encountered; the question to be asked must be "is the analysis based on recent and relevant information or on the way things used to be done?"

(iii) Appraisal methods should contain criteria that represent important work behaviours or outcomes as indicated by the job analysis. They should not be biased

14

towards ability to handle trivial aspects of the job.

(iv) Whatever criterion measures are used, they must be reliable. What this means is that if an appraisal is based on characteristics of the person appraised which are rated idiosyncratically by the appraiser, a similar appraisal is unlikely to be arrived at if a different appraiser were to carry it out. We are all too familiar with the extent to which the unreliability of tests may limit their validity. Just the same restrictions apply to any form of appraisal.

(v) Persons who provide the appraisal must be clearly qualified to do so. They must have a thorough knowledge of the job, the opportunity to see the individual doing that job, and expertise in interpretation of what is seen.

(vi) People should be evaluated on the extent to which they fulfil the requirements of the job rather than on how well they perform relative to other employees.

Who appraises and how

As I have already mentioned, the traditional appraisal model, and the one which is likely to be generally adopted in relation to educational staff, involves a superior conducting some form of face-to-face appraisal interview which will be based upon the achievement of past goals and the setting of new ones. There are, though, other formats available and other possible sources of appraisal.

Dealing with the second of these first, we can look beyond supervisory appraisal. It is probably best that we should: as studies such as that of Barrett (1966) show, supervisors' evaluations tend to be based more on how well they **think** a job should be performed rather than on how well it is **actually** performed by a person. Latham and Wexley (1982) see such appraisals as less reliable and valid than ratings by colleagues of similar status; in general, one's peers have more job-relevant information than do other sources to make an evaluation. The other main source is, of course, the person themselves. Bassett and Meyer (1968) investigated self-rating in a large company; only the employee completed an appraisal form. They found that it led to decreased defensiveness, but most importantly, discussions with managers based upon self-appraisals more often resulted in better on-the-job performance than did the traditional superior-subordinate appraisal. Apart from these obvious benefits, we might also expect this form of appraisal to be particularly appropriate to some forms of special needs posts where no one person can possibly have a clear view of the individual's overall work and where often their "superior" lacks their own specialist skills.

An alternative approach to the usual M.B.O.-based appraisal interview lies in the use of "behaviourally anchored ratings" (B.A.R.S.) (Smith and Kendall, 1963). These are really an extension of what many special education staff are readily familiar with - behavioural observations. Unlike behavioural observations, though, B.A.R.S. are not necessarily limited to what has actually been observed in the past, but to the kinds of behaviours which might typically exemplify good, average or poor performance in the varying dimensions of a job.   The techniques involved in developing these actually render the manager more familiar with what is really involved in a job.   I have introduced the concept and techniques to a group of special school heads who have subsequently applied them successfully to evaluating the per-formance of their own staff;   the use of appropriate behavioural anchors clearly has applications in evaluating the performance of special needs staff. A more full account of the methods involved may be found in Casio (1982).

Training

This is a topic looked at in some detail by Alvin Jeffs in Chapter 3 and is the subject of recent longer texts (e.g. Sayer and Jones, 1986).   Continued professional growth is clearly vital for anyone working in the field of special educational needs when the state of knowledge and ways of working are themselves altering and expanding.   Dubin (1972) has suggested that all professionals possess a "half-life", the period after training when they have become roughly half as competent as they were when newly qualified to meet the demands of their profession. The greater the rate of change in the professional's area of specialism, the shorter will be his or her half-life.

The traditional means of training in special educational techniques was the one-year course leading to an advanced qualification.   For most this was not a prelude to working with children with special needs but a means of updating old knowledge, developing new skills and preparing for a new - usually promoted - role.   Now, as Ivor Ambrose's chapter in this book makes clear, this route has altered and with the new funding arrangements set out in D.E.S. Circular 6/86 we are likely to see considerably less emphasis on substantial release for courses. This is to be applauded if it enables teaching staff to develop skills and knowledge over the whole of their careers, thus reducing the risk of out-living their "half-life";   it is important, however, that staff members themselves should have some part in identifying their developmental needs rather than having training imposed upon them in the hope that to do so will somehow improve them in spite of themselves.

Self-managed professional development does not, of course, exclude feedback from more senior management; neither, though, does it rely solely upon that source. Any self-directed development programme for special needs staff involves four stages (Rosenfield, 1985).

(i) **Assessment of own learning needs.** This starts with an analaysis of just what the job entails, and an assessment of competencies in relation to that analysis. Sources for such an assessment will include line management, self-assessment ratings, review from one's peers and feedback from clients: parents, colleagues in other schools, pupils themselves (see Irvine Gersch's chapter in this book).

(ii) **Selection of goals and objectives.** For this purpose, brainstorming may be useful. After this, particular goals can be set, e.g. "I need to know more about microcomputer software for use with slow learners in mathematics"; "I need to develop skills in observing children's play"; "I should acquire skills in assisting children with phonological difficulties".

(iii) **Consideration of alternative learning methods.** We all learn differently. Some people can adequately gain considerable information from books and articles and put these into practice. For others, short workshops where they can sharpen old skills and learn new ones provide a more useful forum. Obviously, the kind of learning experience chosen will vary with what has to be learned as well as with individual styles and performances. Ainscow (1984) has pointed out that team-centred curriculum development provides an ideal means of staff development; for the special needs specialist in a mainstream secondary school, this may be achieved by active involvement in subject department planning. At the other end of the scale, there may be occasions when a longer course of study or research in another institution, probably coupled with practical school-based activity, will be more appropriate to an individual's needs.

(iv) **Evaluation of professional growth.** This is, of course, something that the classical appraisal interview should set out to achieve. However, because it uses some form of supervisory appraisal, it is essentially a "parent-child" transaction: whether the appraiser is "nurturing" or "critical", the essential position adopted is one in which the appraiser assumes and is granted superior qualities of judgement. I have just used terms from Transactional Analysis (Berne, 1964); the managerial "life position" which is likely to be adopted is all too often one of "I'm O.K. - let's see if you are". In any self-assessment, though there needs to be a degree of objectivity; it is not enough to say "I enjoyed that workshop", or "I met some interesting people on that course". We can distinguish between **progress evaluation** - how well you are getting along your chosen developmental path - and **outcome evaluation** - the extent to which you have changed in terms of knowledge and skills. These outcomes can be further subdivided into -

(a) the extent to which you have achieved your objectives; **and**

(b) the extent to which achieving these has had an impact on your performance as a practitioner.

There is little question that with the introduction of GRIST (grant-related in-service training), the opportunities for special needs teachers to create a coherent and continuous professional development programme will be increased. Any such programme cannot exist without job analysis and appraisal, just as neither of these should be considered unless training opportunities are readily available. The crucial element in all this will lie in the extent to which any or all of these are used coercively or as a means of personal growth and enhancement. Time will tell.

Multidisciplinary issues

So far we have concentrated upon teaching staff. We cannot, however, view them in isolation; as moves progress to integrate into mainstream schools pupils who might formerly have been placed in special schools, so we see a variety of non-teaching staff moving into the ordinary school. Whereas a typical secondary school might until now have had only one or two staff members - such as a laboratory technician - who had pupil contact yet were not teachers, now we see increasing numbers of staff with other professional allegiances and assumptions. These may be based in the school on a regular or even permanent basis, and thus effectively become part of that school's staff, or may visit the school with varying degrees of frequency, their advice and decisions possibly influencing the ways in which children are taught and the working practices of staff. In the former group we may find N.N.E.B. - trained nursery nurses, speech therapists and possibly phsyiotherapists; they may also be represented in the latter, as may school medical officers, social workers, educational psychologists and a variety of other therapists: occupational, art, movement, music.

By definition, members of multidisciplinary teams belong

to different occupational groups; as such they will have been socialised into membership of and identity with those groups, and will use different knowledge bases. More importantly, they are likely to see a given child's difficulties from the perspective of their discipline. Whilst "education" may be defined in terms of curricular outcomes for the teacher, a physiotherapist may have locomotor treatment goals which are given precedence over educational ones. Neither is right or wrong; each simply has his or her own priorities.

One approach to team building is the blurring of role boundaries. Within a department, the intention may be to create an interchangeability which enables one person to do another's job with minimal trouble and disruption. In the case of multiprofessional teams this is probably not the best approach. Cockerill (1953) has pointed to the need for each multidisciplinary team member to have a strong sense of his or her occupational role; the important features are that each should demonstrate good practice and should recognise that one another's unique contributions add up to a total treatment package for the child. What can get in the way of this is the use of differential attributions. One of the ways in which individuals seek to understand what goes on is by identifying the underlying causes of the behaviour of those around them. Thus they attribute causes to their own behaviour and to that of others, to their own failures and successes and to those of others (Forsyth, 1980). Usually, their own failures are seen to be the result of environmental or situational factors (e.g. Johnny in my group isn't progressing in reading because there are no books at home / his parents never read to him / he was minimally brain damaged at birth / I don't have enough time to work with him one-to-one, etc.), whilst others' failures are more likely to be attributed to internal factors or personality traits (e.g. Johnny isn't progressing with Mrs. Jones because she's disorganised / she doesn't like him / the educational psychologist won't countenance the idea of dyslexia / Mrs. Jones isn't interested in implementing individual programmes). When this happens, it is vital that such attributions should be aired and clarified in a non-threatening way, or they are likely to lead to self-righteousness and isolated ways of working.

It is important also to consider the organisational aspects of multidisciplinary teams. Because they represent ground-floor attempts to coordinate the work of separate agencies, some members of those teams will have line managers who are not only outside the school but who have little knowedge of work with children or of education in general. This can lead, when agency priorities differ from those of the school (e.g. in the way members of that agency work with children, in the way in which they allocate their time), to a conflict of loyalties for someone based in the school but accountable also to an outside supervisor. For this reason, it is important that those with leadership responsibilities should not leave team members to "get on with it", but should ensure that their relationships with such people as chief speech therapists and chief physiotherapists are good and that each understands the priorities of, and constraints on, the other.

It is important also to understand the dominant occupational groups from which a team member derives and the assumptions which they make about their domain of influence. Writing principally for social workers, Payne (1982) advises "doctors react badly to anything which suggests that they are not alone responsible for deciding treatment for their patients . . . Teachers feel similarly about curricula, and this sometimes causes problems in assessment centres or community schools" (p.105). Social workers also have ideas relating to their own expertise and its application. Such ideas usually go along with training and real skills; unfortunately, points where one person's skills run out and another's take over are usually difficult to identify, leading to potential conflict. The answer is not to deskill individuals by encouraging everybody to regard everyone else's opinion as equally valid on every topic, but to encourage them to understand the forms of training and expertise that their colleagues possess and, more importantly perhaps, the assumptions that they make concerning their application. Techniques for this are available, although space does not permit them to be elaborated here. I have looked more fully at aspects of team development (Knight and Bowers, 1984) and manuals directed towards this theme are available (Woodcock and Francis, 1981).

Time management

With an increasing emphasis on the supportive and consultant element in special needs work, the question of the effective use of time becomes particularly significant. As I point out in Chapter 5, there are a number of major changes which have to be made when the special needs specialist moves from a separate classroom and timetable to an internal or external support role, servicing and assisting the work of colleagues within one school or a group of schools. Not least of these is a complete revision not only of the way in which they spend their day but of how they schedule their time from day to day and over a longer span. Without some systematic method of allocating time, it is only too possible for an individual's day to become a series of sporadic visits, for there to appear to be never enough time in the day, and for little actually ever to be done.

The management of time has become a priority for many

people in leadership positions: so much so that considerable sums are spent annually on "personal organisers" of one kind and another. Whole texts (e.g. Reynolds and Tramel, 1979) have been devoted to the subject; clearly there is space here only to make a few brief suggestions.

Firstly, the organisation of materials, records, notes, etc. should receive priority. If things have to be moved around, this should extend to the car also. An efficient filing system from which documents can easily be retrieved is a must; the catalogues of office supply firms can provide a lot of useful ideas. For those using microcomputers for much data storage and retrieval, it is possible also to use them to provide a review of the week's schedule and of impending deadlines for such things as reports, course information, etc.

Possibly the hardest transition to make confronts the person used to working within an externally-imposed time framework, such as that of the school, who finds him or herself operating as a regional special needs support teacher/consultant. Possibly there are a number of schools where direct client contact and involvement has been established, others where links are being made, together with a variety of associated agencies which have to be considered, contacted and informed. It is all too possible for that person to misdirect energy and time. A number of strategies are probably of use in ensuring that time is used with a degree of efficiency:

(i)   Draw up a list of specific tasks to be completed in a given time period (a month, a term). Draw up a list of priority. Define the amount of time to be given to each on the basis of this. Try to avoid "job-hopping" by allocating significant blocks of time to each priority area.

(ii) If you have a large project with which you are involved, such as assisting a school in developing a concerted approach to special needs within its walls, separate out the component tasks into small, manageable areas. Assign each one a completion date and try to ensure that this date is met.

(iii) Always reserve enough time for a particular activity. Don't try to cram four major tasks into a day which is already spoken for with three. Probably all four will suffer and along with them your credibility.

(iv) When working alone on such activities as writing reports, devising materials, preparing in-service activities, etc., make an effort **not** to act on other matters which may occur to you. Make a note to give them your attention when you have finished the job in

21

hand. Similarly, try to avoid distractions such as ringing telephones; if you have no one to answer for you, promise to call back unless the call is crucial.

Many of the above comments apply equally to those who have no line management responsibility and to those in leadership positions. Self-management and the management of others have much in common. It is important to remember, however, that so much of what is written on time management relates to how individuals or groups organise their time rather than on the quality of the activities to which they devote that time. The principles of Sexton and Switzer (1978) can be applied here. They were looking at head teachers in particular, but their ideas are equally relevant to anyone who has freedom to decide how their time should best be applied in fulfilling a role which has many facets. From this standpoint, time allocation can be divided into three levels. The first, involving **maintenance functions**, applies to all aspects of a job which ensure that it ticks along. Maintenance functions are the normal routine activities of the day. For the class teacher there are many of them: checking the register, making sure that equipment is available, marking books and so on. Similarly, the support teacher may have programmes to prepare and progress records to complete; a major maintenance function, however, may simply be listening to others and developing trusting relationships with colleagues. At the second level are **critical** or **crisis functions**. These involve dealing with all the issues which arise unexpectedly or only semi-predictably. They can distract but they can also raise adrenalin levels; some managers never get beyond this point, and many teachers' days are spent on maintenance functions liberally interspersed with critical/ crisis activities. The top level is that of **professional goal functions**. These involve activities such as strategic team planning, reading journals and professional literature, evaluating new materials and assessment methods, and so on. Whatever they are, they differ qualitatively from the earlier two in that they carry the job forward not merely in terms of moving on to tomorrow but in terms of growth and change.

One way of analysing the use of time in this way is to break down a working week into half-hour components and then, on a timetable sheet, to log the activities undertaken and the level at which they can be categorised. With this information, where top level activities are inadequately represented, new goals for the expenditure of time may need to be set.

When things get too much

Teacher stress and teacher burnout are becoming increasingly important issues. When large numbers leave the profession, it can be - and often is - explained in terms of stressful conditions and resultant "burnout". Farber (1984) has documented this in relation to teachers; it has though, become a much researched area throughout a wide variety of occupations (Fried et al, 1984) for a variety of compelling reasons, among them the substantial amount of time that most people spend at work, the importance of work as a means for fulfilling personal aspirations, and the individual health and corporate productivity implications of work-related stress.

In reviewing the relationship of service delivery models and organisational roles to stress in teachers of children with special educational needs, Forman and Cecil (1985) note that special education teachers with a resource or consultancy role experience greater stress than do those with self-contained classes. It is difficult to make general statements about sources of stress and their effects on individuals, because what to one person is an energising and challenging situation may be a confusing and depressing one to another. Variables such as constitutional vulnerability to stress, cognitive appraisal of stressful events, personality type, other events in a person's life and the availability of coping mechanisms such as social support, are likely to influence the way in which a given individual will respond to such potentially stressful conditions as pupil disaffection or rejection, colleagues' lack of interest, supervisors' criticism or parents' antagonism.

Although stress and burnout are often synonymous terms, Farber (1984) has argued that burnout in teachers is not the result of stressful conditions by themselves, but of having no support in dealing with these conditions from any source: management, colleagues or even family or friends. Stress does not necessarily lead to burnout unless it goes unrecognised and undealt with. It can be spotted in schools as a whole "when enough teachers spend their lunch hours denigrating students, complaining about administrators, regretting their choice of career and planning for new ones" (Farber, 1984, p.325). It may in fact be too simplistic to talk of burnout as though it is an entity in itself, despite the fact that we have all encountered teachers who appear to have little left to give, whose hearts are not in their job, whose disillusionment and cynicism are all too apparent, and who appear touchy and irritable in most things that they do. Meier's (1984) work has suggested that burnout as a condition is strongly linked with depression; it may simply be a work-induced or work-prompted depressive state.

What can be done by the individual or by those in management positions? Stress is pervasive in most organisations; this chapter is concerned with those delivering special needs services, however, and it is relevant to look at the sub-elements of work experience and stress which may account for responses which reduce individuals' motivation and performance.

The stress components of particular significance for special needs teachers are most likely to be:

(i) **Role expectations conflict.** Here stress is generated as a result of a mismatch between a person's own expectations of a role and the expectations which others have of the same role. The special needs teacher operating as a support resource within one or more schools is likely to be particularly prone to this. He or she may have a clear idea of his or her own job, but others may expect something quite different. An example would be the person with an advisory/consultancy brief who is still expected to withdraw pupils for individual coaching and is criticised overtly or covertly for not doing so.

(ii) **Self-role conflict.** This can generate stress when there is a gap between the way people see themselves and the way they are required to behave. The caring child-centred teacher, whose main satisfaction lies in a continuing relationship with a defined group of pupils, is likely to experience this if required to change to a supporting or consultant role.

(iii) **Role isolation.** This occurs when an individual feels that those occupying other roles, and with whom she or he interacts, are psychologically distant. It is a particular problem for the member of a minority profession - the teacher in a hospital, the speech therapist in a school - but may also occur when a special needs teacher feels that his or her main concerns are not those of colleagues.

(iv) **Role erosion.** This is likely to be experienced in an organisation that is redefining roles and creating new roles. Where somebody has a job which they have built up - the head of a special school, the special class teacher in an ordinary school - and they see that job and its components as under threat, then they are likely to experience stress.

(v) **Role ambiguity.** When people are not clear about the expectations which others have of them, whether due to poor feedback or poor understanding, then this is likely to occur. Role ambiguity has been linked with low job satisfaction, a sense of futility and low self-confidence. Yet it is characteristic of many people attempting to provide special educational services, who will frequently report that they are not sure just what is expected of them.

(vi) **Role overload.** When there are too many expectations, however clear, then role overload will be experienced. Marshall and Cooper (1979) categorised overload into "quantitative" and "qualitative". The first refers to having too much to do, the second to work that is difficult. Either may occur for the special needs teacher; quantitative overload is more likely to be found, though qualitative overload may occur expecially when training has been inadequate or insufficient.

(vii) **Resource inadequacy.** This refers to a person's feeling of having insufficient resources to perform his or her role effectively. It may be due to a lack of material or equipment, a lack of personnel, insufficient information, or even a lack of sufficient knowledge on their part.

(viii) **Role stagnation.** Finally, it is important to remember that as people "grow into" the roles they occupy, become familiar with them and master most of their demands, they may eventually risk becoming "stale" in their work. Linked with this, and exacerbating the problem, may be a reluctance to take on a new challenge even if offered the opportunity. The feeling of "being in a rut" can itself generate dissatisfaction and reduce effectiveness. For this reason, it is important that time limits be agreed for individuals taking on new projects and that responsibilities should be stated at intervals within teams and organisations.

In conclusion

This chapter has concentrated particularly on some of the issues which those in leadership positions in schools and local authorities might usefully bear in mind in developing new methods of service delivery for children with special needs. The most expensive, potentially the most volatile yet also the most crucial resources that they have to manage are the people who deliver those services. An inappropriate selection decision, an ineffectual training programme, an ill-conceived performance appraisal or inadequate appreciation of the prevailing circumstances in the workplace can all prove extremely costly in terms of time, money and personal energy.

It is not easy to define what a "special needs teacher" does; in Chapter 8, four people with differing roles illustrate a working day. In a sense, they provide us with the bare bones of a job analysis. Other chapters will look further at the changing role of the special educational needs professional; it is important, though, to remember that other human resources than those contractually employed are potentially a crucial component of special educational provision. Parents have considerable knowledge of their own child's development and, as Allan Sigston emphasises in Chapter 9, can provide a powerful learning resource. This chapter, though, has concerned itself with some of the prosaic areas of awareness which are important to those with responsibility for the management of professionals. In the following contributions, we have the opportunity to see how others view the components of human resource management at a time of change for special education.

Chapter Two *

NATIONAL INITIATIVES IN SPECIAL EDUCATION TRAINING: INTENTION AND IMPACT

Ivor Ambrose

The Background

The changing national context of education

Responsibility for the education system as a whole, including of course aspects of special education, is exercised at both national and local government levels. It is therefore only to be expected that initiatives should arise, originating from each sector of administration, which are formulated in order to implement the respective policy objectives of central government and local education authorities (L.E.As). The intention behind many an initiative is usually fairly clear: the impact, however, may or may not be accurately predictable.

Central government, being ultimately accountable through the ballot box for the national framework and legislative structure of so many services - such as education - which affect our daily lives, has access to a wide range of sources from which to draw information and advice, as well as being susceptible to influences and pressures upon it, in developing policies and initiating measures to put them into effect. Some of the factors which contribute to policy initiatives in the national context of education are concerned with changes occurring in our society to which the education system must respond. These include such economic and social factors as industrial recession, unemployment, cuts in public expenditure, lower national birthrate statistics resulting in falling rolls in schools and a surplus of qualified teachers, the changing balance of need for teachers in primary and secondary schools, teacher-recruitment requirements in relation to the age structure of the present teaching force, reduced expenditure and provision in the higher education sector coupled with the re-shaping of the initial teacher education and training system, and many more.

Some influences of national policies

Philosophical and political influences are also significant in determining how the education system should operate.
Comprehensive or selective secondary education is only one of
the many major issues linked to the philosophical tenets of
differing political administrations. International perspectives, research and evidence from constant appraisal of
the schools and post-school sectors of education, especially
through the work of H.M. Inspectorate, broaden the information base from which government may draw in planning
educational innovation.

Special education - and the training of teachers for it
- are subject to these wide-ranging factors. In the
mid-1970s many of the problems of effecting massive reduc-
tions in the number of students entering teaching and the
closures of a high proportion of teacher training institutions were also being faced by other countries across the
world. Moreover, it is no coincidence that integration of
handicapped pupils into ordinary schools became a growing
issue of major significance in several countries of Europe at
about the same time as the 1975 legislation in the U.S.A. on
'mainstreaming' and the inclusion of Section 10 in our 1976
Education Act. In the U.S.A. the 'Civil Rights' movement,
rather than specifically educational pressure, was the
dominant influence precipitating the mainstreaming legislation and there were similar, if not so strong, pressures in
other countries.

Initiatives in planning for progress

Some national initiatives operate at the level of organising areas of the total information base. Investigation is
important in this connection, and the setting up of the
Warnock Committee of Enquiry into the Education of Handicapped Children and Young People was an example of this kind,
following a long tradition of previous enquiries into other
aspects of education. Consultation, too, with various
educational and other bodies, including of course L.E.As, is
a recurrent feature of central government practice. Notable
initiatives of this nature have been the creation of the
National Advisory Body (N.A.B.) to advise on public sector
higher education and the Advisory Committee on the Supply and
Education of Teachers (A.C.S.E.T.). Following A.C.S.E.T's
advice which stemmed from its discussion of proposals for
improving the professional training of student teachers, the
Department of Education and Science (D.E.S.) in 1984 took a
controversial interventionist step into initial teacher
training by setting up the Council for the Accreditation of
Teacher Education (C.A.T.E.). With its brief to monitor
professional aspects of the system and recommend to the

Secretary of State whether a course of initial teacher training should or should not be recognised for the award of
qualified teacher status to its successful students,
C.A.T.E's role in operating D.E.S.-designated criteria
affects directly the content and nature of initial training
courses for the teaching of pupils with special educational
needs as well as all other initial training courses. The
most significant initiatives of all are those which provide a
focus for current debates on major policy issues and lead to
legislation. Examples of these have resulted in the various
Education Acts, some of which have had direct or indirect
implications for special education, such as that of 1970
which brought junior training centres and the new E.S.N.(S)
category of handicapped children into the education system,
the 1976 Act which in Section 10 required L.E.As to educate
all handicapped children in county or voluntary schools -
except in certain defined circumstances - from a date to be
determined by the Secretary of State, and the post-Warnock
1981 Act which abolished statutory categories of handicap
(until then the foundation of the special education system
since the 1944 Act) and replaced them by new procedures for
determining and meeting pupils' special educational needs.
Some legislation is prescriptive, setting out what shall
be; some is enabling, designed to allow appropriate agents
to implement its objectives. In the U.S.A., for instance,
the legislation on integrating handicapped pupils into
ordinary schools was prescriptive (though President Ford
said it promised more than it could deliver) whereas our
legislation, as is often the case where L.E.As' roles are
central to the practical working out of its objectives, was
enabling. Legislative initiatives necessitate successive and
lesser initiatives to develop and support them, such as
regulations, circulars and administrative memoranda, many of
these being issued after consultation between officers of the
D.E.S. and interested parties. On these related initiatives,
and the extent to which those to whom they are addressed by
the D.E.S. respond effectively, largely depends the quality
of the process by which the intent of an enabling national
policy is translated into impact on the educational system. A
further dimension of this process lies in the promotion and
monitoring by the D.E.S. of new ways of working, contingent
upon new legislation of other initiatives, in cooperation
with L.E.As, institutes of higher education or other
agencies, with the aim of piloting and/or fostering good
practice. Consultations, courses, conferences, notes of
guidance, financially-assisted projects or funded research
and other similar devices may facilitate this process in
which D.E.S. administrators and H.M.I. become involved.

Centralisation and decentralisation

It is generally agreed that our education system benefits from the dual control and influence of both central and
local government. The two agencies have, for the most part,
traditionally exercised their complementary roles well enough
for there to be no popular clamour for a totally national or
local education service. What is not always so readily
agreed, however, is where the balance should lie for the
control of one to end and the other begin. Demarcation
issues may well be particularly sensitive if central
government appears to L.E.As to be intervening in areas which
they have come to regard as their own preserves. Problems
tend to become exacerbated in times of national economic
recession and financial stringency, when L.E.As' initiatives
may be limited by the need to decide on which areas of
educational expenditure to cut in order to meet their
priority commitments within a reduced rate support grant
(R.S.G.). At the same time, central government, holding the
national purse-strings (albeit of a tight purse), may be
tempted to withhold some funds which might otherwise have
been distributed in a higher R.S.G. and use them to finance
its own national initiatives aimed at meeting new needs,
weaknesses or areas of neglect in the education system as
identified by central government.

National initiatives and financial support

The growth of financially backed national initiatives in
recent years has been a steady one. The educational priority
areas projects of the 1960s, urban aid and inner-city
partnership schemes of the 1970s, and the more recent
secondary curriculum projects, including that for low attain-
ing pupils, have all involved L.E.As, selected by various
criteria to benefit from central funding for specific purposes. The current centrally-funded education support grants
continue and widen this trend to influence schools and
strengthen their curricula directly in the areas of nationally determined priorities.

Essential to the optimum implementation of curricular
developments to meet new priority needs in schools is sound
supportive education and training provision for teachers at
both initial and in-service training (INSET) levels. Initial
training, as a nationally controlled and financed sector, can
be and has been reformed relatively quickly by D.E.S. actions
on numbers of students, closures and amalgamations of
institutions and influencing the academic and professional
content of courses. These have affected special education
training as well as general. From the establishment of new
courses training teachers of mentally handicapped pupils in
the 1970s, to deciding what action to take on A.C.S.E.T's

30

advice in 1984 to phase out such courses, the responsibility has been within the remit of the Secretary of State. The criteria for approval of initial teacher training courses set out in the annex to D.E.S. Circular 3/84, now being implemented by C.A.T.E., include the requirement that aspects of course work concerning pupils with special educational needs in ordinary schools should in future feature suitably in all types of courses.

However effective the impact of Circular 3/84 might be, the likelihood is that for the rest of the 1980s newly trained teachers entering service may only make up about two and a half per cent of the total teaching force per annum. If, therefore, any major impact on practice in school through training to meet new needs is to be achieved, it can only be by INSET involving teachers already in the schools. In the sphere of INSET, however, the balance of control has lain very largely with the L.E.As.

In times of plenty INSET can flourish and new needs can be met by those L.E.As with a positive approach to a professional support service for their teaching force, including access to national and regional courses as well as local ones, though standards of provision at the best of times have always varied widely between L.E.As. During the financial stringency of the past decade, however, many have cut the number of teachers seconded to D.E.S. approved long courses which, through the pooling system, were the main source of financial support offered nationally for INSET. Besides their inability or unwillingness to provide their twenty-five per cent of secondment costs to match the seventy-five per cent available from the pool, some L.E.As closed their teachers' centres, reduced budgets for local INSET courses and withdrew financial support for teachers attending courses outside the local authority boundary. For special education training, which has relied very heavily on INSET provision, much of it at national or regional level since so few L.E.As are well enough staffed to be self sufficient in this area of their support services, these trends were a considerable obstacle to progress. It is not surprising that the mandatory requirement for teachers of the blind and deaf to be specially trained was seen by many as an enviable safeguard for these areas of special education INSET when the rest seemed too uncertain and vulnerable to L.E.As' economies.

It has no doubt long been a source of frustration to successive Secretaries of State, and some L.E.A. officers too, that funds intended to finance INSET and negotiated into the rate support grant allocations to local authorities might end up, in the event, being spent on something else. Local authorities' financial autonomy, established for laudable reasons in many respects, has not made it easy for any Secretary of State to put a case to cabinet colleagues for more money to be made available for INSET as a means of

31

raising standards of teaching in the schools when there was no way of ensuring that the intent would be met and the money so spent. Even if central government was prepared to fund the provision of more INSET in teacher training institutions there was no certainty of the impact this would make on schools or even whether L.E.As would enable teachers to attend.

The D.E.S. initiative in the late 1970s, when reorganisation of initial teacher training was in progress, to allow two ninths of teacher training resources in the institutions to be used for INSET, led to a substantial increase in provision. New courses in both special and other areas of education, many award-bearing, were mainly designed and run by those members of staff who could be made available to do so. Their first requirement was to write a course acceptable to a validating body which could then be advertised so that interested teachers might apply. Diplomas and higher degrees flourished but the benefits to schools and their pupils were not easily discernible and most L.E.As had no significant role except in deciding whether to grant-aid their teachers who participated in the courses. Available provision far exceeded the amount L.E.As would support with teacher secondments, but not the demands of teachers themselves, and the result was a rapid growth of part-time courses mostly requiring evening attendance. For special education, this accelerated the trend towards generic courses rather than the more specialised approach that had characterised most full-time long courses. A part-time course tended to recruit teachers with widely differing experience and interests in special education whose common factor was in living within reasonable travelling distance and wanting an award-bearing course.

Despite some brave efforts to use part of the two-ninths resources on school-based INSET by staff in a number of institutions, they were not sustained very long and the award-bearing courses prevailed as the preferred mode for institutions largely because it was administratively easier to count teachers enrolled on a course than quantify and account for staff time and resources spent on school-based activities. In Scotland the schools benefited more directly from the comparable INSET initiative of the Scottish Education Department which, responsive to the compelling arguments of geography and the small number of institutions, devised an acceptable administrative.and accounting formula for institutions to collaborate with L.E.As on consultancy and school-based activities, resulting in a different kind of impact.

When the 1981 Education Act set a new framework for re-structuring the whole system of special education, shifting the emphasis from categorisation of handicapped children and prescribing education to meet individual special needs - wherever possible in ordinary schools - it was clear that a training initiative centred on those teachers in ordinary

schools with major responsibility for pupils with special
educational needs would be necessary in order to support the
policy. As the date for actual implementation of the 1981
Act drew near, the time was ripe for a national initiative in
INSET capable of offering relevant training possibilities for
a range of priority areas which the existing channels did
not. Out of this context sprang the In-Service Training
Grants Scheme (D.E.S. Circular 3/83) which became a particularly significant development for special education training.

The In-service Teacher Training Grants Scheme - D.E.S. 3/83

Intention

As the growing need for a major boost to INSET, in order
that some impact might be made on practice in schools, became
more widely felt both locally and nationally, and the once
widespread antipathy towards the idea of specific funding by
the D.E.S. seemed to fade, the In-Service Teacher Training
Grants Scheme (D.E.S. Circular 3/83) initiative for priority
areas of training was conceived. D.E.S. press notice 194/82
on September 1st 1982 announced the government decision to
introduce the scheme to take effect in the following
financial year. Circular 3/83 itself, giving full details,
was not issued until 31st March 1983.

Some aspects of intention concerning a national initiative are made explicit, for example in press notices or
circulars, but others can only be surmised. The new scheme
was undoubtedly a breakthrough in INSET - a vehicle of
government intervention - offering a novel and additional
dimension to a system which had evolved in ways providing a
wide variety of long and short courses but not being capable
in existing circumstances of responding promptly to new
national priority needs, as perceived by the Secretary of
State, in such a way as to affect schools and their pupils
directly.

The major features of the innovation were:-

1. The pooling system grant rules were modified to include
    courses of twenty days' minimum duration up to a year,
    thus offering a more flexible framework for the new
    developments.

2. The four priority areas identified for training (math-
    ematics, management of schools, special educational needs
    in ordinary schools (SENIOS) and pre-vocational educa-
    tion), together with the amount of money made available
    to support them (6.3 million for the period April 1983 to
    August 1984), were under the control of the Secretary of
    State.

33

3. The cooperative central/local government aspect of educa-
    tion was acknowledged both implicitly and explicitly by
    the kinds of procedures adopted for implementation, e.g.
    proportional shares of the grant to be spent on each
    priority area were suggested but L.E.As were given
    freedom to exercise virement across the areas if desired
    though adherence to the suggested weightings was to be
    expected in general.

4. "The main purpose of the scheme" read Circular 3/83, "is
    to give direct financial assistance to local authorities
    when serving teachers are released for training on
    designated courses in any of the . . . priority areas
    specified."   Since financial assistance was in any case
    already available through the pool when teachers were
    seconded to approved long courses, it was the particular
    terms attached to this initiative which made it especial-
    ly significant viz. (i) only full-time teachers in
    permanent employment with five years' service would be
    eligible for release; (ii) the notional amount of grant
    allocated to each L.E.A., calculated in relation to its
    school population, from the £6.3 million available would
    be payable only to help meet the salaries of teachers
    employed to replace other teachers sent on designated
    courses.   The great financial inducement was that the
    grant would be paid at ninety per cent of approved salary
    expenses, not the seventy-five per cent rate for normal
    poolable courses.   Additional minor expenditure such as
    course fees and teachers' travel costs were reimbursable
    at seventy-five per cent; (iii) centres servicing the
    four priority areas were specially designated and the
    Secretary of State's discretion was to be exercised only
    in respect of these although, exceptionally, L.E.As were
    free to put a special case if desired for some other
    course to be approved.

5. Paragraph 16 of the Circular stated: "It is the Secretary
    of State's intention under the scheme to secure an
    increase of in-service training in the four priority
    areas."   It was not, therefore, to be an alternative to
    or replacement for existing courses but to be an addition
    offering new possibilities.

6. In essence, the advent of Circular 3/83 widened the scope
    of INSET long courses from being largely a system of
    almost totally "off-the-peg" award-bearing offerings
    tailored by institutions and validating bodies for
    teachers with various personal motives seeking a course
    which their L.E.As might or might not support, to include
    D.E.S.-designated courses in nationally-determined prior-
    ity areas of training to service L.E.As' requirements for

managing their provision in ordinary schools for pupils with special educational needs. The bespoke nature of this development indicated the L.E.As as direct clients of the institutions and thereby gave them opportunities for consulting and collaborating in both identifying the requisite elements of courses and contributing complementary expertise to them, relevant to the responsibilities of the experienced teachers being nominated by the L.E.As to attend.

Setting up the new courses

Although the four priority areas of training covered by the new scheme shared common elements at the launching, they quickly diverged in development according to the several requirements, specific intentions and possibilities of their subjects. For mathematics, both new and existing courses of varying lengths catering for four different categories of teachers (including those of low attainers in mathematics in secondary schools) were eligible for designation as approved centres; for management of schools, one-term and basic courses of twenty days minimum duration for heads and senior teachers were specified, utilising the D.E.S./Regional INSET mechanisms. Each of these areas was allotted one-third of the total funding. Pre-vocational education and SENIOS shared the other third equally, and also the need to set up entirely new courses across the country since there was no network of suitable existing ones. A six-week course pattern was prescribed for pre-vocational education: for SENIOS, a one-term course or sandwich pattern equivalent.

The rubric for SENIOS amplified the general intent of the Circular, outlining the specific purpose of the course, i.e. follow-up to the Warnock Report and the 1981 Education Act, and also set out the guidelines by which the courses were expected to operate. These were very significant, as all the courses had to be newly-devised and submitted for D.E.S. approval. The indication of the kinds of teachers for whom the scheme was intended, the expectation of close consultation between providing institutions and participating L.E.As in designing the courses and the outline of the three major areas of course content to be addressed, provided a useful working basis for all concerned in mounting and operating the courses.

In practice the rubric was sufficiently suggestive without being too prescriptive and it triggered off some very imaginative responses. Fifteen SENIOS centres were designated in time for the issue of the Circular, geographically spread across England from Exeter to Newcastle-upon-Tyne and Lancashire to London. Despite some delays, occasioned by necessary but time-consuming administrative procedures, which resulted in Circular 3/83's not being received by institutions and L.E.As until early in April 1983 for a scheme commencing that same month, one of the centres was actually able to run a summer-term course.

Each of the fifteen institutions was invited to send a course tutor and a representative L.E.A. member of its course planning committee to a one-day conference held at the D.E.S. headquarters in July. This provided a forum for discussing the Circular's implications for SENIOS and a launching pad for shared ideas and experiences on progress in producing courses, many of which were currently recruiting and planned to begin the following term.

Management of innovation is seldom without problems, and in interpreting and responding to the Circular both institutions and L.E.As had some to face. Not least, for institutions, was the absence of any funding for the provision costs of courses. Existing resources had to suffice, though course fees could be charged to L.E.As and used towards course expenses. Inevitably some institutions, despite having a strong interest and expertise in SENIOS, were unable to offer a course on those terms. For some L.E.As, accustomed to fairly lengthy procedures when considering their teacher-secondments for INSET, the late issue of Circular 3/83 and the relatively short timescale in which to use the money it offered presented a difficulty. Furthermore, it was predictable that few would be in the position of already having a considered policy for SENIOS which included one-term secondments for a group of carefully selected teachers, ready to leave their schools for a term at short notice with their temporary replacements standing by and the heads of their schools nodding approvingly. Nevertheless, despite these and numerous other obstacles encountered in setting up the new mechanisms rapidly to implement the new initiative, the high level of enthusiasm and cooperation of institutions' staff and L.E.As' officers ensured that almost all the fifteen centres were able to recruit and run successfully at least one course, and in some cases three, during the four-term 1983-84 period covered by the Circular.

Impact

Responses to the national initiative

Many studies of policy implementation have analysed the process in various ways. Barrett and Hill (1984) stress its political nature involving negotiation, bargaining and compromise on the part of those involved in the chain of action. Weatherley and Lipsky (1977) outline the role of "street level bureaucrats" in relation to the reform of special education in the U.S.A. who may constrain and distort the implementation. Easton (1979) uses the term "gate-keepers" for those key figures who facilitate or block, innovate or modify and generally develop or manipulate the process, and identifies their differing bases for action. There is a general recognition that the impact of a policy will be greatly influenced by many individuals responsible for or affected by its implementation, acting within their own constraints to protect or enhance their own interests. Certainly, however inspired a national initiative might be, its benefits are invariably capable of being negated by mishandling.

Welton (1982), referring to the 1981 Education Act, remarks that the function of legislation is not only to enable good practice, but to promote that practice, encouraging, and where necessary requiring, administrators and professionals to work in prescribed ways. The function of Circular 3/83 was similar. Allowing for the differences between institutions, L.E.As and the individuals in them, there can be no doubt that the initiative had the effect of capturing the imaginations and enthusiasm of a significant number of people involved in setting up the courses. This impetus transmitted itself to teachers on those courses and quickly began to influence work in schools. Levels of consultation, cooperation, joint planning, sharing of personnel and resources between institutions and L.E.As in the organisation of courses, reached unprecedentedly high levels, resulting in valuable INSET experience not only for the teachers on the courses but also for the tutors and L.E.A. officers concerned. New possibilities had dawned for all, and were certainly being fulfilled by some, viz:

a) INSTITUTIONS found the construction of a one-term course in collaboration with representatives of L.E.A , without reference to an academic validating body and frequently without the privilege of student selection, to be a very demanding but rewarding exercise.

b) L.E.A OFFICERS were in an even more novel situation. Given their preoccupation with day-to-day responsibilities in the organisation and management of the schooling system, their collaborative sessions with staff or institutions, identifying and discussing agreement on objectives and how to achieve them, could be somewhat taxing. The familiar option of leaving matters to the institutions and then being critical of their shortcomings was not a defensible one: this was an opportunity to help steer the INSET to local teachers.

c) TEACHERS, by and large, responded with a kind of duality which reflected their participation not only in an individual capacity but also in a representative one on behalf of the staff of a school and/or a group of

37

teachers seconded by their L.E.A. to a course for a particular purpose.

d) Even SCHOOLS from which course members came were in some instances a responsive element from the outset and were involved as part of the process by which the course and school-based follow-up was planned.

Naturally, not everything clicked smoothly into gear everywhere at the start and many a tutor can recall course sessions badly matched to course members, L.E.As less careful than desirable in selecting teachers for secondment, teachers inadequately briefed and too many people at all levels having unrealistic expectations of the courses and the roles of their products. Nevertheless, by the time Circular 4/84 was issued in May 1984, renewing and increasing the financial allocation to continue the INSET training grants scheme for another year, much had been learned and achieved, making it an undoubted milestone in INSET progress. The increased funding meant that more teachers could be seconded and eight additional centres were designated.

Impact on the courses

Many aspects of the courses reflected the L.E.A.-as-client nature of the scheme. Some L.E.As took their partnership-in-close-consultation role very seriously and offered some key personnel from their special educational needs advisory support services for schools on secondment to their local course for tutorial and liaison purposes, along with the group of teachers being seconded from their schools. Psychological, welfare and remedial services were also made available to assist with course work and arrangements for cooperation facilitated by joint L.E.A./institution staffing of courses. Membership of courses naturally illustrated L.E.As' own priorities in training for SENIOS. One L.E.A. sent ten heads of primary schools on the first local course; others gave priority initially to secondary school teachers. Institutions serving several L.E.As negotiated on whether to provide for both primary and secondary phases within the same course or have separate ones. The contents and programmes of courses varied widely, whilst generally remaining reasonably faithful to the Circular's broad guidelines, because of the differences in the kinds of course membership and the per-ceived priorities of the L.E.As concerned with a particular institution. Since many courses were very practical the opportunities available locally for visits to and liaison with L.E.As' schools and support services were a major influence. A few courses aimed to train trainers and equip members to lead school-based or L.E.A. shortcourse INSET.

A question sometimes raised in the initial planning of

courses was whether an institution should recognise a teacher's satisfactory completion of the one-term course by granting a certificate and whether for those teachers who developed a taste for further study such a certificate might count as a credit for some remission within an advanced award. This question, of course, raised issues about the nature of course work, whether there might be assessment procedures and negotiations with the validating body for whichever advanced award was being considered. The training grants scheme was not concerned with validation of courses for award-bearing purposes, but such an idea was not specifically ruled out. Several institutions decided to award their own certificates and in two cases, by further extension of the institution/L.E.As' negotiations which produced the course content to making proposals to the validating bodies, these particular courses became acceptable as units in modular diplomas. Nor did the ripple effect end there. Some L.E.As revised their own short course programmes to complement the local training grants courses and some were prepared to second more than their quota of teachers, exercising virement across their total financial allocation for all the priority areas of training of accepting the normal seventy-five per cent pooling grant for the excess numbers instead of ninety per cent. As institution/L.E.A. collaboration progressed there were signs of it carrying over to other INSET courses run by the institutions.

Outcomes

Many facets of impact arising from the training grants initiative have already been touched upon. It is always difficult trying to judge in any generally agreed way the overall effects of INSET given the multiplicity of contributory ingredients to the mix such as in this case quality of the personalities and the process involved in the tutors' and L.E.A. officers' planning of course content, preparation and selection of course members, the kinds of practical and theoretical work required of them, the capacity of a member to utilise knowledge and skills gained on a course productively with pupils in school and the follow-up offered by L.E.A. resources.

It would be naive and totally inappropriate to judge the merits of the scheme solely by looking for results through the short-term follow-up in schools of teachers who had completed a term course. Nevertheless, there certainly were many examples of direct outcomes of various kinds, suggesting that this mode of INSET could operate quickly and to good effect on the schools when well planned. There were products of 'training trainers' courses who actually did participate in running L.E.A. and school-based short courses for other teachers; there was much writing of new teaching programmes

and preparation of materials for particular groups of pupils
based on knowledge gained from courses; new organisational
developments fostering greater cooperation between departments of a school, school and L.E.A. support services, school
and parents etc. went alongside the important but unmeasur-
able factor of teachers' greater confidence and enhanced
self-concept in feeling more knowledgeable and better able to
understand the complexities of meeting pupils' special
needs in the ordinary school setting.

Evaluations of courses took many forms and reflected to
some extent the degree to which the initiative had captured
people's imaginations. Apart from in-house evaluations by
tutors incorporating views of their course members, heads of
school used and L.E.A. officers involved, there were length-
ier studies of a single course or several as part of some
higher degree students' work and one by the National Foundation for Educational Research (N.F.E.R.) for the D.E.S.
Appreciative comments and supportive action towards follow-up
in schools were significant features of L.E.As' responses.

A two-day invitation conference funded by the D.E.S. in
April 1985 brought together course tutors, representatives of
some L.E.As and N.F.E.R. to share experiences and discuss the
scheme's developments and main outcomes over the two years
since its inception, relating these to the nature of
follow-up of courses, evaluation and pointers to the future.
Circular 3/85, renewing the scheme for a further year,
followed in June. It contained an addition to the rubric for
school management training courses, basic and one-term, which
stated, "The Secretary of State hopes that training courses
of both kinds will pay attention to management responsibilities which may arise in relation to children with special
educational needs." Follow-up conferences and meetings of
course members were held both by institutions and, for their
own teachers, by L.E.A. advisers responsible for SENIOS. One
major centre (in terms of the number of courses it had run)
held a day conference in March 1986, just three years after
the issue of Circular 3/83, for the large number of teachers
who had passed through them. It illustrated what had been
achieved in that relatively short period and reflected many
of the successful features already stated: in particular the
collaborative nature of the enterprise involving institutions, L.E.As' officers, teachers and their schools
colleagues. Despite many workaday problems in their schools,
the inevitability of some disappointments, set-backs, aspirations unfulfilled, finances sought but unobtained and other
realities of the educational scene which caused some teachers
present to have less to show in the short term for their
INSET than others, there was no doubting the testimony they
bore to the value of the scheme and its impact on work in
their schools.

Outlook

The strengths and weaknesses of a national initiative must to some extent be determined by one's point of view. In this case institutions with resources available to mount courses were enthusiastic; those without were not. It is arguable whether a financial allocation for provision might have produced a better staffed and resourced network of courses. Some L.E.As would undoubtedly have preferred cash without strings to spend as they wished; others were glad to make the most of the scheme offered. Funding of a scheme on a one-year-at-a-time basis creates uncertainty about its future and may to some extent inhibit good forward planning by both L.E.As and institutions. The one-term duration of courses, though generally welcomed, could be seen as too restrictive by some since the same amount of money might have trained more teachers on shorter courses. However the strengths and weaknesses of the scheme are regarded, its intent was certainly achieved in several respects:-

a) It provided a new dimension to INSET which offered possibilities and opportunities taken up to good effect in some centres and therefore capable of such in others.

b) It identified for special education a new area of training need which was not being met and to which many people in L.E.As and institutions could relate, finding common interest for productive cooperation.

c) It raised the esteem and level of importance of training for SENIOS to a national priority.

d) It offered a financial incentive to L.E.As to use the opportunities presented and plan the management of their INSET for SENIOS more systematically in conjunction with designated institutions.

In the final analysis, of course, an enabling policy initiative can only encourage high quality of response, not guarantee it.

National initiatives in special education training are a continuing process and one becomes overtaken by another. The impetus of any new scheme cannot last indefinitely, since the context in which it operates is constantly changing. It must be carefully monitored and as the circumstances leading to its inception alter, reviewed for decisions to be taken as to whether it should be just left to continue, reinforced by other measures, adapted or possibly withdrawn in favour of something better if it has served its purpose. Important questions to be considered as part of that process for this particular scheme are how many teachers trained on a one-term

SENIOS course are needed? What kind of balance should be struck between these courses and other special education training and how can it best be achieved?

Whatever answers emerge to those questions, the 'fait accompli' of the scheme is that a cadre of one-term trained teachers with SENIOS responsibilities is now established in the schools of many L.E.As. The long term impact of the national initiative will largely depend on how effective they become within their L.E.As' strategies for SENIOS and within the day-to-day constraints of management in their own schools. The outlook will certainly be brighter if the hope expressed initially in Circular 3/85, and followed up in 1986, that school management courses should pay attention to management responsibilities relating to children with special educational needs is really needed and acted upon as this is a current gap in INSET.

Government plans for far-reaching changes in the financing and administration of INSET will necessarily affect special education training. As the effects of the 1985 major initiative which introduced T.V.E.I. related in-service training, financed by central government through the Manpower Services Commission become more widely felt, the likely implications of the proposed re-structuring of INSET in 1987 will become clearer. With these initiatives leading to the enactment of new legislation aimed at the creation of a new set of ground rules as envisaged in Circular 6/86, it will be for those with responsibilities at all levels in the area of special educational needs once again to assess the potentialities of the system that results, making the most of new opportunitites as some have done with the INSET grants scheme to tackle new problems in training for special education. The achievements afforded by the INSET grants scheme will have been a useful stage on the way.

Footnote

Since this chapter was written, ideas on centralisation and decentralisation issues in education emanating from the "radical right" of politics have created new pressures for shifting the balance of control further away from the L.E.As. It remains to be seen whether central government power will be used to substantiate these ideas.

Chapter Three

APPROACHES TO STAFF DEVELOPMENT

Alvin Jeffs

Why Staff Development?

The discussion concerning special educational needs provision since the setting up of the Warnock Committee in 1974 has highlighted the fact that policy changes need to take place in the context of the 'whole school'. As the Fish Committee indicates:

"Every major decision about the organisation, content and methodology of education has significant impli- cations for those with disabilities and difficulties which may influence the extent and nature of special educational needs and the means necessary to meet them." (Fish, 1985, p.6)

Responses to the "significant implications" involve not only changes in resource allocation. There are also aspects of attitude and teaching style implicit in any effective response to Warnock's recommendations and subsequent legal requirements.

It may be that this will involve "changing attitudes, arrangements and approaches in schools, colleges and the community" (Fish, 1985, p.5) or it may be that Warnock's giant leap will, in fact, become the small step presaged by the 1981 Act. Whatever the outcome, the classroom teacher, the support teacher and their heads cannot remain unaffected. Whether as a "restricted" or an "extended" professional (Hoyle, 1975) s/he will need to respond in an informed way. The consideration of staff development is essential if the debate is to be informed and responses more than short-term reactions to the L.E.A. requirements. It is also essential because of the nature of educational institutions, especially in times of change.

Gray (1975) indicates that educational organisations, like all organisations, are built upon members' needs and aspirations. In terms of exchange theory (Homans, 1958),

43

membership of a school or support service may be seen as involving a continual negotiation, and commitment exists only insofar as members receive an acceptable reward that meets these needs and wishes. In Gray's terms, membership may be "active" (seeking specific, valued returns) or "passive" (content with receiving no negative returns).

Within this context, the art of good management is to facilitate the "renegotiating" of this "psychological contract" with individual members so that each continues to be committed and changes are assimilated in terms relevant to each member's conditions. Thus, a second basic reason for considering staff development policy is that it provides a necessary means by which this negotiation can take place.

Can Traditional Management Theory Help?

There is an understandable scepticism with regard to the application of management theory to educational settings. The words "manager", "subordinate" and "training" do not sit easily alongside the concept of the extended professional and many schools which are both stable and responsive to change do not work in these terms.

A few authors have recently considered staff development in the specific area of special educational needs (Hodgson, Clunies-Ross and Hegarty, 1984; Galloway, 1985). It is, however, generally true that the literature on staff development is large but unread by teachers (Oldroyd, Smith and Lee, 1984).

It is the intention of this chapter to draw out and illustrate how some strands of traditional management theory provide a basis for conceptualising and structuring staff development within any school or support service. Two recurring themes throughout this examination will be the importance of job satisfaction and the perceptions of needs upon which all organisations are built.

In many ways much management theory is familiar in its vocabulary and thinking. One quotation will certainly ring true to educators in the 1980s:

> "The acquisition of job knowledge and preparation for further responsibilities must be integrated into the general work and life experience of the individual. It is ineffective to train a person in some skill, technique or area of knowledge and return him to a work environment where his new ability is manifestly not required or rewarded." (Sidney, Brown and Argyle, 1973)

Traditionally "training" has, in the words of the Industrial Society (1964, p.12) been seen as a:

> "process of changing attitudes or behaviour through
> instruction, demonstration, practice, planning
> experience or other techniques."

This definition may serve as a basis upon which to consider
the process of staff development, though **with one crucial
modification.**

Accepting the nature of organisations as "the patterned
activities of a number of individuals" (Katz and Kahn, 1966),
and schools as pre-eminent examples of negotiated membership,
staff development may be seen as a process of **people changing**
their knowledge, skills, attitudes.

Without individual control over professional development
and without full participation, staff development will be
little more than cosmetic. From this point staff development
will be taken to mean:

i)   a form of job enrichment and self-fulfilment;
ii)   a vehicle for 'whole school' development;
iii) the responsibility of senior management to initiate;
      but
iv)   a **contractual** process that takes account of individual
      personalities and learning styles.

Staff Development in Context

Head teachers and heads of support services have not
always seen individual staff interviews and long-term professional development programmes as part of their role and the
Warnock Report itself was not at all specific on this point,
indicating only special educational needs elements within
management courses (Warnock, 1978). Any attempted development of such a policy also needs to be set against a
background that is not conducive to the whole-hearted
acceptance of new and time-consuming processes.

Education is a profession where rewards tend to be
"normative" (i.e. based upon esteem, respect and satisfaction) rather than "remunerative" (Etzioni, 1976). It is also
a profession where demands have increased as social status
has declined, resulting in a high degree of work-related
stress (Dunham, 1984). Typically within this profession,
development has tended to be passive, relying heavily upon
courses and isolated INSET initiatives often focused outside
the school and usually conducted by personnel external to the
school membership.

However, while the constraints are clear, opportunities
also exist. Indeed, they need to exist if a static
profession is to continue to achieve job satisfaction and
respond creatively to national and local requirements. At
the same time the staff development programme can form a less
emotive and more mutually beneficial procedure than that

often implied by the term "teacher appraisal".

Any head setting out to implement a coherent staff development policy with regard to special educational needs might usefully consider that policy as one of **dialogue** between senior management and individual staff against the backdrop indicated in Figure I:

Requirements

(What all teachers in the 1980s should be aware of)

The 'spirit' of Warnock
The 'letter' of the 1981 Act
Local LEA initiatives, requirements and support networks

Opportunities

(The benefits to be derived for individuals and institutions)

More effective classroom performance
Greater job satisfaction
Access to support facilities (internal and external)
Development of new skills
Contribution to developing school policy

Constraints

(Factors likely to reduce motivation and hinder discussion)

Lack of time
Limitations imposed by availability and quality of support and INSET personnel
Increasing demands across the curriculum
Anxiety arising from the 'teacher appraisal' debate
The need to encroach into non-teaching time
Varying perceptions of special educational needs and INSET

Figure I

The backdrop to a S.E.N. staff development policy

Principles and Processes

Another fundamental way in which management theory
relates to teaching lies in the vocabulary and structuring of
the process of training, which typically -

 i)   seeks to **identify needs**;
 ii) takes into account **individual learning styles**;
iii) works towards the **structuring of objectives**;
 iv) focuses on the implementation of the programmes on a
      contractual basis;
      and
  v) builds in an **evaluation of outcomes**.

This combination of long-term aims and short-term
objectives is a familiar one within special educational needs
work. Its application and value to staff has not been so
carefully considered.
A more detailed examination of the five points,
illustrated by reference to the staff development experience
of Peter, a peripatetic support teacher, may serve to
indicate how the process appears in practice. In Figure II
on the next page we see an appraisal form for completion by
the head teacher. A fuller description of the exercise can
be found in Jeffs (1984).

Identification of Needs

Whatever the precise format the staff development policy
takes, the identification of needs is almost certain to end
as a compromise between the "tactical" (i.e. the needs of the
organisation) and the "organic" (i.e. the needs and hopes of
the individual) (McCormick and Tiffin, 1975).

To this discussion the head or member of senior
management brings -

 i)   a picture of what is needed to provide a balance within
      the institution;
 ii) knowledge of extrinsic pressures that are currently
      making demands of that institution.

Each teacher brings a knowledge of -

 i)   why they are in the organisation;
 ii) how they see their role;
iii) what they see as rewarding developments.

Although this stage can be completed **during** an interview, it is often useful for staff to complete a questionnaire beforehand so that the interview can make the best use

47

Please indicate your ratings on the 7-point scale beside each aspect.
The 7-point rating should go from strong (lefthand side) to weak (righthand side) with 4 as "satisfactory".

Administration of
group assessments   ... ✓.. ... ...

Individual assessments .. ✓.. ... ...

Devising work
programmes   ... ✓.. ... ...

"Advising"   ... ... ✓.. ... ...

Counselling pupils   ... ✓.. ... ...

Counselling parents   ... ... ✓.. ... ...

Parents meetings   ... ✓.. ... ...

Contact with staff
(professional)   ... ✓.. ... ...

Contact with staff
(personal)   ... ... ✓.. ... ...

Organisation of
resources   ... ✓.. ... ...

Record-keeping   ✓.. ... ...

Background knowledge
of pupils   ✓.. ... ...

Providing information
requested   ... ✓.. ... ...

Maintaining balance
between loyalty to
school and
loyalty to service   ... ✓.. ... ...

Liaison with outside
Agencies   ... ✓.. ... ...

Balance of the time
between 'Advising'
and Teaching?   ... ... ✓.. ... ...

(the last two lines are for any extra categories thought to be relevant)

Figure II An appraisal of Peter's performance by one head with whom Peter worked

of time. It is equally useful in encouraging staff to articulate their feelings and ideas.

The teacher's own appraisal can be supplemented by a similar appraisal by head and/or a colleague chosen by the teacher.

The overall plan agreed following the appraisal inter-view and a discussion of appraisal forms completed by Peter, his head of department (Area Tutor) and a 'client' head are shown in Figure III below:

"Advising" (including:
   reports
   in-service contact
   recommendations)
Contact with staff
  (professional)
Time allocation
  (ability to say "no")
	AREAS THAT COULD USEFULLY BE EXAMINED FOR INCREASED EFFICIENCY

Counselling parents Parent meetings Liaison with outside agencies	AREAS DEALT WITH WELL, BUT MORE OPPORTUNITY WOULD ALLOW EXPERIMENT-ATION AND DEVELOPMENT
Group assessments Developing materials	EXCELLENT. DEVELOPMENT NEEDED IF WORKING OUTSIDE PRESENT SETTING

Figure III The programme for action

Aspects of learning style

Figure IV on the following page indicates how Peter rated various forms of in-service development. In this instance the staff member used past experience to highlight the most suitable **means** by which to achieve the objectives.

The eleven modes of learning are in no way comprehen-sive. For example, many schools might wish to consider video and discussion or the use of an interaction analysis. The basic list is possibly best produced by a brainstorming staff session.

By this stage there is likely to be a clearer idea of

Forms of training	A	B	C
"coaching" by colleague	..10.	.....	.....
discussion - once or twice	...4.	..4..	.....
- regular	...9.	.....	.....
being given task (trial and error)	8	.....	.....
direct instruction (1.1)	...1.	..1..	.....
specific staff meetings	...3.	..3..	.....
reading	...2.	..2..	.....
setting 'targets' for attainment/discussion	...7.	.....	.....
course(s) - local - e.g. Bristol	...5.	.....	.....
working with someone else	...6.	.....	.....
seeking advice of outside expert	..11.	.....	.....

In column A please place in rank order the methods of training you have found most useful in the past.

(number 1 to 11)

In column B please indicate the four methods you would most favour for developing any future new skills.

(number 1 to 4)

In column C please tick if you think that the form of training you have indicated in column B for the 4 priority areas of training would be possible for you to undertake within the next two terms.

Figure IV   **Peter's preferred methods of in-service development**

perceived needs and the methods of meeting them, together with an acceptable time-scale. Using a formal schedule of this nature allows a detailed picture to be built up for a large number of staff as well as providing the basis for individual interviews (Jeffs, 1986).

Structuring Objectives

No staff development interview should end without structuring of measurable objectives. In some cases the number of objectives will be small. In the case of Peter the discussion had indicated a willingness by both himself and his head of department (Area Tutor) to develop a clear framework detailing both short- and long-term objectives.

The detailed development plan is shown in Figure V. It was further agreed that a regular - termly - monitoring would take place and specific meetings arranged with the possibility of short, interim, meetings if necessary.

Time consumption was highlighted earlier as a possible restraint. The first three stages have indicated some, comparatively small, time expenditure on the part of the teacher; a little more by the head of department.

In Figure VI we can see how Peter's experience might fit into an organisation of 48 staff where no one is responsible for more than six staff interviews, while all staff have the right to request an extra interview with the head or relevant deputy.

Implementation

The value of this type of organised procedure, as Jinks (1979) points out, is that all parties have reference to initial objectives and the methods of attainment are clear.

Thus, Peter's preference for 1:1 instruction was linked closely to a "tutorial" approach. In this case it was with his head of department, although such support might easily derive from a peer-tutoring group within the organisation or sessions with an outside agent, such as a member of staff from a local teacher-training or INSET institution with responsibility (and time) for such work. The role of the outside agency is strongest for those staff who wish to discuss and consider aspects of the job that involve colleagues or areas of perceived weakness.

Evaluation

McGregor (1960) sums up the participative form of training as "basically . . . creating opportunities under suitable conditions for people to influence decisions affecting them"

51

UPGRADING OF EXISTING SKILLS

Training Need	New Work Behaviour	Criteria for "Success"	Learning Process	Timing
Report writing	Producing formal report including assessment and recommendations.	Production of reports acceptable to immediate superior.	Reading and discussion of report format with Area tutor. Assessment in a new school.	Summer term. Autumn term
In-service involvement	Demonstration and talking to teacher groups.	Satisfactory feedback from teacher groups. Satisfactory observation by Area Tutor.	Involvement in courses and in-service days.	Autumn term
Advisory role in regular schools	Increasing discussions with staff.	Own satisfaction.	Development of newly-initiated discussions. 'Post mortem' with Area Tutor. Reading Argyle text.	Through Summer and Autumn term
Time allocation	Providing materials and information for staff to act on. Creating new balance between teaching and staff contact.	Continuing this as part of regular work. Developing method of advising and supporting staff during week.	Discussion with Head teacher and staff. Time logging. Reading texts provided by Area Tutor.	Summer or Autumn. End of Summer term. Beginning of Autumn term

DEVELOPMENT OF UNDER-UTILISED SKILLS

Training Need	New Work Behaviour	Criteria for Success	Learning Process	Timing
Contact with outside agencies	**Setting** up contact with Educational Psychologist, speech therapist, E.W.O.	**Initial meeting** and procedure for contact.	Staff meeting with Ed. Psychologist. 1.1 meeting with speech therapist, E.W.O.	Summer term
Parent meetings	**Addressing** parent group.	Satisfaction of **Headteacher.**	Attend P.T.A. talk by Area Tutor. Discuss material.	Summer term
Counselling parents	**Structuring** counselling session.	**Checklist** largely followed.	Argyle text and checklist.	Autumn term.
Development of materials for 'distance-teaching'	**Compiling** list of materials to be purchased. **Incorporating** recommendations into reports.	Presentation of **list.** **Use of list** for reports	Staff meeting discussion on materials. Visit to Bristol Reading Centre.	Early Summer term

FIGURE V   Peter's plan of action

(p.126).

In making use of participation, the manager "recognises that he is beginning what may be a lengthy process of growth and learning for his subordinates and for himself as well" (McGregor 1960, p.128).

If staff development is seen as part of the process of renegotiation within the organisation, and if the person facilitating this process embarks on a truly participative form, there must be the acceptance of an evaluation of the facilitator's role. In Peter's case the evaluation of his own development was to be in terms of those **verbs** listed under "New work behaviours" (see Figure V).

The facilitator's role was also to be evaluated. The contract in this instance required the facilitator to -

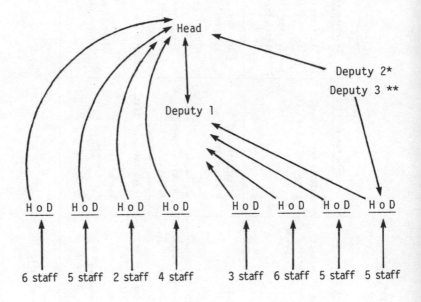

* Deputy 2 opting for development interview with Head

** Deputy 3 opting for development interview with H o D

Figure   VI   **Staff development programme on larger scale**

i)   organise opportunities for Peter to carry out the relevant training activities (e.g. in-service days, staff meetings with educational psychologists and "tutorial" time);
ii) provide relevant materials (e.g. texts and sample reports);
iii) provide appropriate and constructive feedback on each training need (by observation and discussion with relevant heads and teachers).

The form of structure indicated here is only one of a number of formats and one that appealed to both teacher and facilitator.   In terms of both structure and formalisation, arrangements could be significantly different.   For an example of a looser model, reference should be made to Bush, Glatter, Goodey and Riches (1980, p.401 et seq).

Resistance to Development

It would be self-deluding to suggest that all staff automatically greet change and professional development with open arms. As Hoyle (1975) has pointed out, the "restricted professional" tends to see skills as deriving solely from classroom experience, has limited involvement in non-teaching professional activities and rarely becomes involved in in-service work.

How does a staff development policy attempt to cope with this?

There are a number of factors which cast a more positive light on any basically static situation:

i)   **consultation** - in the participative spirit indicated above it would be foolish to introduce a structured programme without full discussion by **all** staff. An in-service session or staff meeting is often a good forum in which to introduce and debate such a topic;

ii) **style of staff development** - acceptance of real participation, of "exchange" and an emphasis upon individual learning styles goes some way towards accommodating the more restricted professional;

iii) **interview styles** - a leader should have a range of styles available from "listen-and-support" (a basically counselling approach) through joint problem-solving (possibly the most creative style) to "tell-and-sell" (a more authoritarian approach which is occasionally accepted by staff who later find value in the training process);

iv) **"passive" staff development** - the very least that a staff development programme can achieve is the prevention of professional deterioration. In this context the most "restricted" member of staff has an opportunity to discuss existing policy, contribute ideas and make observations on her/his own position;

v) **reward systems** - a number of small studies indicate quite clearly that the failure of a school to adjust its reward system in terms that are meaningful to staff correlates closely with teacher dissatisfaction and alienation. An overview of such studies suggests the obvious; unless the institution values the values of its teachers, a very real dissonance ensues. The same study makes the positive point that the opportunity to exercise leadership and further personal learning is a stronger factor within the average teacher's search for job satisfaction than might be assumed (Chapman and Lowther, 1982)

Case Studies

Clearly the example of Peter is atypical in that it represents highly structured staff development within a support service context. Two case studies are now presented in some detail. Although composite studies, in that they represent initiatives in a number of schools brought into a single coherent framework, they serve to indicate how the basic structure can be adopted in different ways at both primary and secondary levels.

Each study is based upon a 'whole school' approach to staff development. In the case of the secondary school, the need to respond to the 1981 Education Act becomes one element in a regular procedure concerned with the total development of each member of staff. In the instance of the primary school, the necessity of a response on special educational needs prompts a concerted effort to develop a format for general staff development.

STUDY A

Setting

A junior school (Group 5), in a suburban area of a major city.

Staffing

Head, deputy, 8 class teachers, 1 S.E.N. unit teacher and 1 part-time ancillary attached to unit.

Staff development format

None at present apart from occasional unstructured and informal discussions with enthusiastic members of staff.
The need to respond to the LEA circular and requirements concerning the implementation of the 1981 Act is seen by the head and the deputy as providing a good opportunity to construct a staff development approach that might be of use on a more regular basis.

Stages of S.E.N. initiative

Step 1

Two terms are designated by head and staff as having a special educational needs focus (this has been used effectively in the past with the examination of literacy and mathematics within the school). The agreed elements include two staff meetings in each term, one in-service day, the use of identified funds for S.E.N. materials and a detailed examination and development of links with outside services by head and deputy.

Term 1

Step 2

An in-service day for all staff, together with infant school staff, representatives from the governing body and deputy-head of comprehensive lower school. The whole staff group is addressed by the LEA adviser for special educational needs on Warnock and the 1981 Act.
Small workshops are taken by the senior educational psychologist, the teacher of hearing-impaired and the remedial support service area tutor. During the first part of the afternoon small staff groups discuss formats for staged assessment.
At the end of the day each member of the junior school staff is asked to identify and write down individual requirements in the light of the day's discussions with tentative suggestions for meeting them.

Step 3

Retirement of a staff member allows the creation of a post of responsibility (Scale 2) for special educational needs liaison and staff development. This is deliberately someone other than the unit teacher to allow a strengthening of expertise within the school.

Step 4

This designated teacher applies and is accepted for a one-term course for S.E.N. coordinators.

Step 5

The designated teacher takes a staff meeting to ask staff what they wish him to investigate during his course.

Step 6

Over a period of three weeks, the head and deputy each meet with five staff to discuss professional developments in detail.
(Both head and deputy use this activity as part of their own agreed professional development.)
The requirements and implications shown on the following two pages are felt to be realistic within contractual hours:

Term 2

Step 7

The designated teacher presents initial working paper ('Warnock, the 1981 Act and my school') to staff.
Specific themes are considered of priority by staff:

   i) extending parental contact and involvement;
  ii) further use of support services;
 iii) use of observational checklists for early identification of behavioural problems.

Step 8

The head teacher asks for a brief, written report on their own investigation with at least one specific proposal for:

   i) school policy in general;
  ii) allocation of funds.

Step 9

The designated teacher returns with school resource file built up during course. During a school assembly taken by the head, the teacher and deputy lead a discussion on the course and future developments identified.
As one outcome of this meeting, two teachers volunteer to join the designated teacher at monthly meetings with other S.E.N. co-ordinators and support teachers.

Teacher	Identified needs	Preferred means of achieving them	H.T.'s commitment
T1	Up-dating knowledge of reading schemes and literacy techniques.	Two sessions with support service at local reading resource centre with follow-up reading.	To obtain two ½-days supply cover for unit teachers. Internal cover arranged for T1 and T2. Head to contact resources centre.
T2 Unit Teacher			
T3	Clearer understanding of needs of hearing-impaired children.	Discussion with hearing-impaired support teacher. Access to support services videos, books and handouts.	To arrange time for discussion in school.
T4	Development of topic work with full range within mixed-ability class.	T4 and T5 to work on a team-teaching basis to develop group work activities and try out taped back-up to adapted work cards. T6 to use mixed-ability groups within class, using materials developed by T4 and T5.	Release of unit ancillary helper once a fortnight to join team-teaching setting. Discussion of programme between head and T6. Head to co-teach with T6 once a fortnight.
T5			
T6			

Teacher	Identified needs	Preferred means of achieving them	H.T'S Commitment
T7	No real needs identified.	Agreed that procedures had to be followed.	
T8	Concern expressed over new referral procedures and lack of materials for under-achievers in maths.	Contact with advisory maths teacher to be made.	Ear-marking of small sum for maths materials recommended.
Part-time ancillary	Long-term interest in becoming qualified teacher.	Willing to work with T4 and T5. Discussion with adviser concerning professional development.	Head to check on possibility of her attending in-service courses. Details of teacher training and O.U. courses sent for.

Both the head and deputy identify similar areas of concern and discuss together the implications and arrangements.

The Head Teacher's Role

Throughout the process the head has acted as a facilitator. By keeping a record of the process he is able to evaluate the outcomes in conjunction with his senior support service personnel. A more specific aspect of a head's involvement with regard to long-term career prospects is outlined by Marks (1983).

STUDY B

Setting

A comprehensive school in a suburban area of a large city.

Staffing

Head, 3 deputies and 50 teaching staff.

Staff development format

Deputy head (pastoral) in charge.
Annual, 30-minute, interviews with each member of staff based upon self-appraisal form and culminating in projections for professional development during forthcoming year.

Stages of S.E.N. initiative

Step 1

Clarification of responsibilities - discussion between head, deputy and head of special needs support department.

Deputy head (pastoral) to have responsibility for 'whole school' policy initiatives with regard to special educational needs and relevant INSET policy.

Head of department to have day-to-day responsibility for professional development of department's two full-time staff, two part-time staff and subject teachers who help in department. There will also be the responsibility for seeing that at least one S.E.N. specialist teacher attends other departmental meetings in an advisory capacity. The head of department will also have responsibility for advising the deputy with regard to policy matters.

Step 2

Deputy and head of department present three discussion documents to senior management group:

61

   i) "Meeting educational needs in ordinary schools"   (NUT
      1984)
  ii) Synopsis of Warnock Report
 iii) Synopsis of 1981 Act and LEA responses

Step 3

Senior management group (with head of department) identify
what they regard as basic staff development needs at two
distinct levels:

   i) the whole school staff   - essential knowledge
                                     - possibilities for INSET
                                       support
  ii) S.E.N. departmental staff   - essential knowledge
                                     - possibilities for INSET
                                     - further study in area of
                                       S.E.N.
                                     - development of techniques

Step 4

In-service day arranged and three brief papers distributed
to all staff:

   i) summary of Warnock Report
  ii) summary of LEA policy (1981 Act)
 iii) details of support facilities (external and internal)

Step 5

In-service day:

a.m. "Warnock and the classroom teacher" (LEA principal
      educational psychologist)
      "LEA assessment procedures and local responses to the
      1981 Act" (mixed-faculty groups led by senior member
      of support services)

p.m. Departmental discussion groups consider implications
      for their department
      Departmental policy document produced in rough by each
      department under headings:

      This department's response to the S.E.N. debate
      Possible staff development
      Reactions to the possibility of co-teaching
      Ways in which we could use S.E.N. department support

Step 6

Synopsis of departmental report circulated to all staff

Step 7

Specific developments arising from in-service day:

  i) Member of S.E.N. department gains place on one-term course (to act as an identified link between S.E.N. department and subject teachers);
  ii) Voluntary in-house course organised to cover wide range of S.E.N. considerations (sensory impairment, curriculum modification and literacy skills);
  iii) Allocation of £100 to develop staff resource library and resource files (copy of "Educational implications of disability" (Male and Thompson 1985) purchased for each department and orders taken from individual staff);
  iv) Series of four detailed policy meetings between S.E.N. department staff and representatives of educational psychological service, hearing-impaired service and LEA adviser;
  v) Arrangements made for members of staff to visit and assist in special needs department;
  vi) Co-teaching built into next year's timetable within Humanities department to fit in with block time-tabling and Humanities department request;
  vii) Head of S.E.N. department applies for one-year secondment course (Diploma in Special Educational Needs);
  viii) One member of Craft department and one member of Home Economics apply for part-time B.Ed. (Special Educational Needs).

Step 8

Two specific questions are included in the next staff development appraisal form:

  i) "In what way have you been able to follow up the in-service day ideas **within your department?**"
  ii) "In which ways can or should the school provide facilities to enable you to follow up initiatives in this area?"

Step 9

A one-term pilot study of co-teaching between the S.E.N. department and Humanities indicates a favourable response from subject staff, some reservations by one of S.E.N. teachers and an interest from two other subject departments.

63

Step 10

Head of S.E.N. department is asked - as part of his full-time course - to evaluate the implications of co-teaching in detail and indicate options for future policy.
Clearly, in the secondary study a significant amount of time involved in the staff development exercise involved non-contact time. It is unlikely that a large organisation can follow through such a detailed programme without reliance upon departmental meetings and courses. In fact, it would require a great deal of any educational institution to pursue an effective policy in this field without some reliance upon non-contact time.
At this stage it seems fair to say that effective responses in terms of discussion, liaison and INSET assumes time given to meetings and activities beyond the nine-to-four time-span. Having said this, the degree of involvement within Study 2 does recognise the constraints of time and other commitments on many staff, together with the importance that special educational needs developments hold for specific members of staff.

*   *   *   *   *

In Conclusion.

Staff development has not traditionally been an area where all schools and support services have felt obliged to adopt a coherent, long-term and detailed policy. It has been the intention of this chapter to indicate that the construction of such a policy need not be difficult.

It assumes a careful identification of long-term aims and individual objectives. It needs to take into account individual preferences. It relies heavily upon an understanding of both the limitations and possibilities within an inevitably mixed group of staff. Above all it is likely to flourish where true participation exists.

The contribution that management theory has to make in this process should not be underestimated. For many institutions that do not possess a clearly articulated staff development policy, coping with the general and specific issues arising from the special educational needs debate may provide an opportunity to carry out some detailed thinking and suggest processes that will be equally applicable to other areas of educational life.

Through the process staff may learn, in the words of Margulies and Wallace (1973) that:

"The real learning . . . lies not so much in the
fact that the team has learned to do things in a
different way, but more in that its members have
learned to assess their own patterns of behaviour,
diagnose difficulties in those patterns and
establish new and more effective ways of functioning" (p.103).

Chapter Four

MAINSTREAM SUPPORT WORK - WHAT IS IT ALL ABOUT?

Maggie Balshaw

Introduction

An authority or a school may produce at its own level a
blueprint for change. However, whilst innovation may be
planned with great precision and forethought, change in any
organisation takes a great deal of time and is fraught with
the kinds of difficulty that are documented by Nicholls
(1983). She outlines some of the issues, including changes
of attitudes, changing roles and bringing about new relationships, the loss of certain aspects in which people feel
secure and competent, and the change to practices in which
they may feel, albeit temporarily, less competent. They may
therefore have to tolerate feelings of insecurity and often
take an extra workload. This chapter contends that the
facilitation of the process of innovation with respect to
supporting children with special needs in mainstream schools,
and helping to overcome the difficulties associated with
these changes, should be the fundamental aim of the
mainstream support teacher.

I intend to examine the issues and to suggest some
skills which could assume importance during people's interpretation of others' intentions for them in the overall
blueprint for change. During the last five years I have
gained personal experience in mainstream support work, while
based in a special school for children with moderate learning
difficulties, working with neighbouring schools to develop a
response to special needs. The skills which have been
demanded of me over this period of time are not necessarily
derived from special school teaching experience, but are far
more comprehensive and wide-ranging.

The first part of the chapter deals with the policies
and plans which may be drawn up in order to initiate a
response to special needs; it goes on to look at the changes
which may need to take place in attitudes, perceptions and
approaches, and then provides a more detailed examination of
three major areas in the implementation of plans, people, and

the processes through which they go, and their perceptions of the situation. The second part examines in further detail some aspects of the support teacher's role in dealing with mainstream teachers' responses to the changes required of them. As a result of reflecting on my experiences over five years, I have come to recognise these aspects as being of crucial importance.

Policies and Planning

Whose?

Change may result from an authority initiative or a local response to the challenge to meet special educational needs. Whoever delineates policies and plans may work out in detail structures and a framework for a co-ordinated response, but may not necessarily take account (nor could an authority removed from the scene of the action realistically be expected to) of the personalities involved. How much better is a local initiative able to build into the framework knowledge of the personalities involved?

Why?

An authority may be responding to a much wider demand, perhaps even legislation. A local initiative responds specifically to local needs and can develop ideas more flexibly because of this.

How?

The policies and plans may be carried out in a number of ways, but in order to fulfil the challenge of Warnock and the 1981 Act a whole-school response is often the method suggested. Sayer (1985) stresses the importance, in developing such a coordinated response, of in-service development of everyone together in localities focusing on a pooling of skills. This method is given further support by the Fish Report (I.L.E.A., 1985; 3.16.15) which suggests that clusters of schools should work together, the cluster becoming an important forum for curriculum development, in-service education and staff development.

Change

These plans and policies should lead to change in three areas:

Attitudes

Negative attitudes appear more prevalent than positive ones when special needs are discussed. The pressures felt by the teacher in a mainstream classroom, faced with the prospect of coping with children with special needs and being firmly charged with the responsibility for them, may be a direct cause of these negative feelings. Also contributory can be traditional attitudes towards 'remedial' children, who are often considered in the light of their failures in a working situation, and their successes in a social or behavioural sense, such as disrupting the normal routine!

Perceptions

The idea that an expert will take away a child and 'sort him out', not recognising the importance of the environment in which the child functions most of the time, is the traditional one. The concept that all teachers are teachers of children with special needs, and an awareness of the importance of the supportive, stimulating and socially involving climate of the classroom, are difficult ideas to assimilate and accept, and teachers need support in their attempts to do this.

Approaches to special needs

A positive approach to children with special needs is where the change of emphasis should lead, in terms of looking at strengths the child possesses as well as weaknesses. An identification of what he can do and an ability to seek ways of building on those strengths, whilst at the same time helping to overcome weaknesses in skills he may have, should be the basic aims. Doing as much of this as possible within the mainstream classroom also constitutes a part of the change in emphasis.

Factors in Implementation: People, Processes and Perceptions

What happens between policies and plans and their implementation and therefore, change, can be considered under three headings:

People

Who is involved and why?

In each of the schools involved in working towards a co-ordinated response to special needs there is a hierarchy of staffing. The levels of hierarchy actively involved in

68

this response may influence the speed and efficiency with which changes can be made. In the special school, members of the senior management team should be involved in the support work. In the mainstream school the coordinator ideally needs the active support of the head and, depending on staff size, at least one other senior member of staff, to increase the effectiveness of input and feedback in every department. In the secondary school this involvement of staff from other departments becomes far more complex and depends largely on the way the school is structured for curriculum/subject areas and pastoral care/year groups.

In this way several levels of teamwork may be developed, with senior staff or heads meeting together to plan and organise, and coordinators of the schools also meeting regularly to decide on and implement decisions at that working group's level. Groups of classroom teachers might also meet together. Feedback from each of the groups should be channelled into the others.

Other personnel, such as advisers and the educational psychologist involved in the schools, may be involved in some or all levels of the organisation. Officers of the local education authority may also be included on an occasional or regular basis to monitor and contribute to the proceedings, particularly where support or resources have been requested.

Processes

What happens in the dissemination of information?

In a model which uses information dissemination from a central source, with the structure being based on direction from the top, difficulties are likely to arise.

Decisions about who should receive information may carry hidden messages about recipients' inherent worth to the scheme in general. Contrary to much present practice, all those people actively involved in decision-making processes, at whatever level, should be informed of the rationale behind the guidelines from which they are expected to derive their own decisions. Information passed on by letter or telephone is liable to loss, filtering, watering down, misinterpreting, misunderstanding, and to being left 'pending' indefinitely.

What happens in the sharing of information?

Information shared amongst people and discussed in a group situation has a far better chance of having some real effect on people's actions. Where classroom teachers, mainstream coordinators and heads actually meet together, their views are more likely to be given equal consideration, regardless of their position in the hierarchy. Perhaps still more effective are meetings involving staff from different parts of the hierarchy and from different types of school: sharing and discussing in groups involving nursery and infant teachers, or junior and secondary teachers, or heads and coordinators of all types of school, may be   extremely useful to all involved, giving insights into   others' concerns and enabling a more cohesive approach to special needs to be generated.

Perceptions

What are the perceptions of the following groups?

Headteachers

If the head teachers accept the need for a whole-school response, they will have to appraise the skills already existent within their schools in order to make use of these in the initiative. Hegarty and Pocklington (1982) note that heads often indicated that they had got the 'gist of the scheme', but subsequent events proved that this was not so, and this resulted in difficulties. The head's perceptions of his special needs coordinator's role, and the ways he may support it, are important. His idea of how the support teacher may be expected to work in his school, and the use he can make of such a person in ordering his ideas as to the school's possible response, affects the way the support role is fulfilled.

Special Needs Coordinators

Special needs coordinators are often 'nominated' for the post! They are often lacking in status. It may be that they are not confident in some or many of the skills required of them. What will they be expecting of the support teacher? Are their perceptions orientated towards an expert adviser, or towards a practising classroom teacher? The climate in which they work, and the organisational constraints of their schools, may be fundamental to their ideas of how they can fulfil their role. The support teacher will need to be aware of this and adapt the method of working appropriately.

Classroom Teachers

Do classroom teachers hope to be absolved of responsibility for children with special needs, or are they fully aware of their own responsibility towards them? Do they have a clear picture of what the special school teacher may be able to offer - not necessarily solutions, and certainly not immediate ones, but rather ideas to try out and some fresh insights into the problem?

The Special School Staff

The special school staff directly involved in support work may not be as experienced as the support teacher who is responsible for coordinating the work of the special school in its support role. Are they aware of the pressures faced by mainstream teachers - the sheer pressure of numbers, and other concerns such as expectations of parents and senior staff for 'results', often judged in terms of children's academic success, particularly in written skills? They need to know what is expected of them by mainstream teachers and also be clear in their own minds what is possible, indeed appropriate, for them to offer, in terms of help, support and materials. The mainstream teacher's reception of such an input could be affected by a personal sense of 'failure' in a situation and this may provoke a reaction not anticipated by the special school teacher.

It is not always possible for all special school staff to be directly involved in the support role of the school. Dessent (1984) highlights the tensions associated with what can become a 'divided' staff; he stresses the importance of obtaining commitment, if not practical involvement, of all the staff, if serious problems are to be avoided.

Problems resulting from these perceptions.

What level of understanding of special educational needs do mainstream staff tend to have? This can vary enormously and perceptions of what constitutes a special need may relate to children in the category of the Warnock 2% or to those who have specific learning difficulties at some stage of their school life. Mainstream teachers have been used to the category of 'remedial' children, who by regular withdrawal from the classroom into a small group may have been expected to 'catch up' with their peers; far less familiar is the idea of children who are intellectually quite capable, but have certain pockets of difficulty which may for example cause them to have problems in producing written material (so often the yardstick by which capability is measured), although they have understood the concept and purpose of the work.

Croll and Moses (1985) found mainstream teachers' perceptions of children's difficulties were often ascribed to factors innate in the child or to elements in his home environment, or to a combination of these; it was unusual for a teacher to view a child's difficulties as arising from factors within the control of the teacher or the school.

Many mainstream class teachers state that the issue which most concerns them is not identifying the needs, but dealing with them. They express feelings of inadequacy and incompetence, coupled with guilt feelings about having done 'nothing'. These are often expressed in association with feelings of anxiety about the very able, or middle-of-the-road majority, who may be neglected if there is a shift of emphasis toward children with special needs.

In view of their varying perceptions of the role of the support teacher, what form of service delivery will mainstream teachers expect? This may vary from a sympathetic ear to a carefully prepared programme of work. Hegarty and Pocklington (1982) focus on some of the difficulties encountered in support work and note the possibility of raising the classroom teacher's hopes unrealistically - with disappointment following lack of instant success.

The perception of an extra workload incurred by taking on the responsibility for children with special needs, may colour attitudes to whatever the support teacher offers in the way of methods or materials. Smith (1982) notes that the mainstream teacher may well be questioning whether 'help' means extra work, and that assistance in implementing suggested ideas needs to be provided.

Support Teacher's Role

In the work in which I have recently been involved, I have found the following ten areas to be key components of the support teacher's role:

Listener	Ambassador
Learner	Manager
Counsellor	Facilitator
Confidence giver	Disseminator
Practitioner	Negotiator

Listener

Initially the support teacher's role involves far more listening than bringing in an agenda or advice. Edwards (1985) stresses the crucial importance of 'communication' skills. Amongst these is being a good listener, giving sympathetic attention and responding in a way which shows understanding. Smith (1982), in looking at the role of the remedial teacher as consultant, also notes the importance of listening skills with the question 'Do you listen - really listen?' The ability to listen effectively, showing awareness of what has been said with appropriate expression, gesture and tone of response, is noted by him.

Allowing space and time seems to be an essential requisite; giving the busy mainstream teacher the feeling that there is an importance in what she has to say can be reinforced by the creation of this. The need for this time out of the bustle of the classroom to give her space to think through some ideas, often verbally, is important and it may fall to the support teacher to organise a situation in which this can happen. The mainstream teacher has her own ideas, but allowing time for her to rationalise these thoughts and asking leading questions can be an essential part of the support teacher's role. In clarifying her ideas, the mainstream teacher may at the same time put all the issues in context for the support teacher. At this stage input may not be necessary - certainly not initially. Having sorted out some basic ideas and issues or needs to be dealt with, there may then be an appropriate point to offer some input.

Learner

The changing role involves new skills that are not possessed just because special school teachers are skilful classroom operators. Ainscow et al (1978) became aware, during a pilot project for mainstream support, that changing the special school teachers' role by expecting them to pass on knowledge or expertise, highlighted the need for in-service training of the in-service trainers. The relevant in-service training of support teachers must play a crucial role in equipping them with skills which are not just to do with being skilful classroom teachers. Georgiades and Phillimore (1975) also stress the necessity of preparing the culture in which newly-trained experts are to work. This is only possible by learning about that situation in order to help the teacher alter it, and so improve the environment in which she works. It is also important to learn about the environment in which the mainstream teacher is working, to be aware of its limitations when making suggestions about ways to support children within it, even something as fundamental as the amount of table space children may or may not have for extra materials.

This learning process must be seen as a two-way function involving both special school skills and mainstream skills. Mainstream classroom teachers have a wider familiarity with the full curricular range of experiences to be found in a mainstream school. They also have the ability to manage greater numbers of children on a day-to-day basis, often without other adult help. These are skills which a special school teacher may have had at some stage, but if she has been in a special school for some length of time the normality of a mainstream classroom can be a 'culture shock'. Her perceptions of the level of achievements reached in a special school classroom may be far removed from the mainstream context.

There may be more learning involved for the support teacher in secondary situations, where the mainstream teacher's subject skill base is so pronounced. The support teacher's personal experience is often not extensive enough, nor would it be reasonable to expect it to be, for supporting staff in a range of secondary subjects. Attending lessons is invaluable because, in encountering the subject with which she is not familiar in any depth, the support teacher can almost take on the role of a pupil, experiencing the kinds of difficulty the children themselves have to work through, the discomfort felt leading to a good deal of empathy with their reactions and feelings.

This is a case for interactive learning. Each has a lot to learn; there is a mistaken assumption that it is always the mainstream teacher who is learning. A pooling of all skills on offer is fundamental to the coordinated approach to special needs.

Counsellor

The support teacher is in a position of trust through discussions and is privy to much confidential information about schools. The neutrality of the role is often assumed, and issues fundamental to changing ideas and attitudes often have to do with people and their relationships.

This happens at several different levels. Head Teachers divulge confidential information about their staff and, in evaluating the response their schools can make to special needs, there will be the necessity to discuss with the support teacher the strengths and weaknesses which exist amongst the staff. The teachers' aspirations for their professional development and their head's perception of these may be of crucial importance to developing a whole-school approach.

In discussions with the support teacher, staff voice opinions about other staff, and special needs coordinators raise difficulties encountered in fulfilling their role. Personalities involved in attempting to obtain a whole-school response have an effect on how this may be done. A special needs coordinator often finds a very varied response both to her in her role, and to the whole concept of special educational provision. Staff at various stages in their careers and having previous experiences of innovation, some positive and some negative, may exhibit a whole range of feelings from blind enthusiasm to 'we've done it all and seen it all before - and it didn't work then!' Talking through these issues with the coordinator puts the support teacher not only into a unique position of trust, but also into one which may be dealing with very emotive and subjective areas, where a counselling approach is essential.

The support teacher is often in a position to watch other people teach. Edwards (1985) notes that this needs to be treated confidentially and this is particularly pertinent at secondary level. Subject teachers need to know that observations made in these lessons will not be passed on to those in the school organisation or hierarchy who may make judgements about their performance.

The support teacher must be aware that she is in a very privileged position, having detailed information on a range of confidential aspects in several schools. Any suggestion that this privilege has been abused could severely damage the trust built up between her and other staff in mainstream schools, and its importance should not be underestimated.

Confidence giver

One of the critical issues involved in responding to special needs in the mainstream school is that of teachers feeling de-skilled. Mainstream teachers often express feelings of panic about their inadequacy to deal with special educational needs, and forget the many skills which they already possess.

Ainscow and Muncey (1983), in looking at a whole-school approach and how schools had been able to attain this, identified six factors as crucial for success, one being the need for confidence in the staff that they could deal with children's special educational needs. Smith (1982) notes that a question to be asked is 'have you realised how good you are?' and deals with the issues of de-skilling. He suggests strategies for examining the more successful lessons and relationships for suggestions of different approaches to problem situations; an ability to help the mainstream teacher build on these successes is a rewarding and reinforcing behaviour.

The support teacher needs to emphasise the importance of building on good practice already in evidence in mainstream classrooms, experiences of which the special school teacher may not have had recently, because of the context in which she works. Particularly relevant are those of dealing with much larger numbers of children, offering a wide curricular choice, grouping children so that the more able ones can help to support those with difficulties, and general management of a mainstream classroom.

Feelings of being threatened by the whole situation created by integrating children with special needs, or supporting those children already in the mainstream classroom, need to be taken into account. Because the mainstream teachers often do not understand the implications of this, they need help in building up confidence, and may be reassured that much of their current good practice can be built on.

Practitioner

It is important that the support teacher is seen as a practising classroom teacher. Dessent (1984) highlights the fact that the 'expert-consultant' image is not always an appropriate one. The support teacher is in a position to demonstrate credibility as a practitioner in a number of ways.

An invitation to the support teacher's own classroom is one possibility, giving mainstream colleagues not only a chance to see the special school in operation, but to see the support teacher in her own environment with her own responsibilities. Useful discussions may arise from this about the methods and materials used and how they are managed, the strategies and teaching styles employed for individual differences, and the general organisation of the classroom.

A support teacher who is based in an all-age special school may have had the opportunity to teach children at any age from three to sixteen. In a flexibly organised special school, giving staff opportunities for career development and varied experience, this may have been a routine event. How much more credibility would the support teacher have then in whichever type of school in which she is involved? To be able to cope effectively in a mainstream nursery at one stage, and then contribute meaningfully in a secondary classroom later, enhances the image of a capable practitioner.

In order to allow flexibility of working in supporting special needs, it may well be relevant to offer to take a teacher's class while she works for special needs, or take a group to allow for each teacher to work with a smaller number of children. A practitioner is able to do this, and in doing so to enter a collaborative phase with the teacher whose classroom is being shared, which would be impossible if working on a withdrawal basis.

Ambassador

Dessent (1984) indicates the necessity to play down the role of the special school as an institution of experts. In being an ambassador for the school, the support teacher needs to avoid going into schools with 'answers'. The notion that special schools have 'got it right' and can therefore offer instant solutions needs to be firmly rejected. Hegarty and Pocklington (1982) note the difficulties in coping with mainstream teachers' previous experience of the remedial service in operation. Teachers are likely to equate their perceptions of the remedial service, with all the inherent implications of that, with that of the role of the support teacher. If that is so, then the support teacher will need to be skilled at deflecting this possible comparison.

The special school's expertise is grounded in dealing with small numbers of children, giving specialist help and using materials which are very often unsuitable for use in a

mainstream classroom.   The support teacher should avoid
inappropriate suggestions, otherwise teachers often make
fully justified comments such as 'It's all right for you, you
can do that with only ten children and an assistant - I
couldn't hope to with my thirty and no help!' and 'I can't
cope with things like that, they lose all the pieces!'.

Nevertheless, the special school has much to offer, and
part of the ambassadorial role has to do with drawing
attention to what is available, and its relevance to
mainstream situations.   The support teacher with awareness
of mainstream practice, and sensitivity to potential problems
in introducing special school practice into this, can do much
to develop acceptance of the compatability of the two
approaches.

The support teacher is not only an ambassador for the
school and special school practice, but for other members of
the special school staff, whose initial involvement in the
mainstream schools she may set up.

Manager

Bowers (1980) deals with the issue of the lack of training given to senior special school teachers for their management role, in terms of internal special school management;
with the developing role of the special school as a support
service to mainstream schools, this surely has much wider
implications.   Because primary, secondary and special schools
traditionally have different patterns of organisation, the
extension of the management role to encompass these differences considerably increases the potential for this skill
area.

In the special school, the support teacher's role may
include keeping other members of staff informed and 'with'
the work in principle, influencing management decisions about
who should join the team, assisting other staff to fulfil
their role successfully, making decisions on the appropriate
areas for involvement, timetabling to allow for fulfilment of
outreach commitments, and supporting them through any
difficulties they may be facing.

An awareness of primary school management practice, and
particularly of those issues facing heads of very small
schools in managing for change, is crucial.   The problems met
by heads, who may in principle be willing to organise to meet
special needs, require careful consideration and sympathetic
support.   The contrasting issues faced by the head of a large
secondary school, which may have an inflexible or traditional
management structure, rooted in adherence to examination
syllabuses, separate subject departments, and setting,
involving the time-tabling constraints imposed by all these
factors, call for tactful handling by both the support
teacher and the special needs department staff.

When joint approaches are being suggested involving management issues in different types of school, the support teacher will need to recognise how carefully such initiatives should be introduced to all parties, and the need to take slow and careful steps. The support teacher should not underestimate the amount of exploratory groundwork required, or the number of meetings needed to discuss the management of these initiatives.

Facilitator

Much of the work done, particularly in secondary school, to support teachers can only be achieved with a background knowledge of the complex organisation in which the teachers are working. Hockley (1985) stresses the need to get to know the organisation, physical layout of schools, and staff resources, in order to be able to suggest alternative strategies. Flexibility tends not to be a high priority in timetabling, room and staffing allocation, and yet working with special needs is often all about flexibility; therefore the support teacher's strategies for facilitating some flexibility in the system need to be many and varied.

One aspect of this is suggesting to different levels of the school hierarchy what might be done and how; in the role of support teacher this may be seen as less of an imposition than if a member of another subject department tries to initiate change.

Bringing discussion groups together, involving staff from all the schools with similar concerns, is another way of facilitating effective progress of work. Jeffs (1986) notes that support teachers have stated a preference for working in close relationships with colleagues, in small close networks; the support teacher is ideally placed to organise such groups, which may be invaluable.

Arranging contact between 'unusual' groups of people, crossing traditional boundaries, is another function of this role. For example, the support teacher can, where relevant, involve members of junior schools and secondary schools in discussion groups on topics such as secondary transfer for children with special needs. Groups of primary school and secondary school teachers seldom work together, and much may be learned from this common experience - often with much greater implications than for special needs alone.

Passing messages between working groups and keeping unity of purpose and an overall 'togetherness' in what is being done is also a relevant and important activity for the support teacher. A knowledge of the personalities involved helps in this respect; knowing what approach to take to certain individuals so that messages are received and 'understood' can be crucial.

78

Disseminator

Hockley (1985) discusses the importance of INSET in dealing with the needs of teachers of children with special needs, rather than of the children themselves. The teachers' special needs are those with which the support teacher may be most concerned. Teachers need to become more aware of other sources of support and that the special school is not the only one. The mainstream teachers seldom have the experience of meeting or collaborating with multi-professional personnel such as the educational psychologist, the speech therapist and the advisory teachers for sensory deficits; contact tends only to be through the head teacher.

Authorities vary greatly on what there is on offer to teachers for supporting special needs and seem to vary even more in making teachers aware of what is available to them. The support teacher is in a position to carry out this function.

The INSET role is crucially important, with particular consideration for the professional development of all those involved. Galloway (1985) suggests that teachers have special educational needs, and emphasises the importance of furthering the professional development of staff in this area. Teachers who are growing in professionalism and learning through their involvement in INSET are always seeking to be 'better' in the classroom. Developing their ability to meet special needs is an aspect with which the support teacher should be very much concerned, and the methods employed in this practical and school-focused INSET are more likely to have lasting effects than in-service delivered from a distance.

Negotiator

The role of negotiator can involve such varied issues as sharing classrooms, suggesting strategies, involving parents as partners, choosing meeting places with tact, helping people to work effectively within their organisations, and arranging for staff to exchange roles to encourage flexibility.

Traditionally, mainstream teachers have been accustomed to working in isolation in a classroom behind a closed door. The idea of sharing a classroom may be uncomfortable at best, but can be totally alien and very threatening. Delicate and lengthy negotiations may be required to encourage teachers to share their classrooms in the first place. Thomas (1986) suggests that, to take maximum advantage of sharing a classroom, strategies need to be worked out beforehand on which role each of the adults is to play. This brings into focus questions about seniority, responsibility for lesson content, discipline, etc., all of which are potentially emotive and problematic areas.

In order that no one school is seen to be the 'base' for all that goes on, and so that there is a shared responsibility for hosting meetings and opening doors, negotiating the use of a variety of meeting places may be an important function of the support teacher's role.

Helping people to work effectively within the constraints of their school organisation can also be crucial. A mainstream coordinator often has to attempt to fulfil her role despite the school's internal organisation. This may, by its very nature and traditions, militate against what is being attempted. The support teacher's role here may involve negotiating with the head on behalf of the special needs coordinator, in order that some changes might be made in difficult areas; or negotiating with special needs and subject department staff in order to make organisational changes in a secondary school.

Conclusion

In looking at the ways mainstream support may be carried out, I have attempted to highlight how the process of changing attitudes, perceptions and approaches is fundamental to innovation for meeting special needs. The people, processes and perceptions which lie between the plans for change and their implementation play an important part in how it happens, or indeed, whether it happens.

The aspects directed more overtly are likely to be those that are the results of legislation, changes in authority policy, and from a high level in the administrative hierarchy. The key role played by the support teacher in this process of change is to translate the demand for change into appropriate aims and objectives, aligned to particular localities and people within them, and assist in their implementation. This could be achieved in the ways outlined from personal experience in the latter half of this chapter. The support teacher may not necessarily be based in a special school, but may be part of an area support team or another authority structure resulting from changes of policy after the 1981 Act. However, many of the situations are fundamental to support work, wherever the base, and have relevance in a number of different organisational settings.

The important question arising from this is whether the teacher working in a support role may reasonably be expected to possess the range of skills demanded of her. It is unlikely that previous teaching experience will have provided many of the ten skills discussed. The following questions seem relevant:

Mainstream Support Work - What is it all about?

1. What INSET opportunities for professional development need to be provided to prepare teachers to meet the demands of the support role?

2. What are the implications for authorities in providing the INSET necessary to implement the recommendations of Warnock and the 1981 Act?

Warnock (D.E.S., 1978) stressed the importance of the re-training of teachers to meet special educational needs. Surely in-service provision for the support role comes into this recommendation and, a decade later, authorities need to address themselves to the issue of the special educational needs of their teachers.

Chapter Five

INTERNAL AND EXTERNAL SUPPORT: ROLES AND DEFINITIONS

Tony Bowers

At one time, the term "support" in education was reserved for ladies' foundation garments and surgical appliances used by over-energetic P.E. teachers. Now we find that a lack of "organisational support" is viewed as a cause of teacher dissatisfaction and stress (Cunningham, 1982), "support services", in the shape of educational psychologists, medical officers, educational welfare officers and various therapists, have been defined (c.f. Lindsay, 1983), and a new breed of special needs teacher - the "support teacher" - has sprung up.

We can crudely categorise the type of support that such individuals provide as internal consultancy or external consultancy. The former has tended to grow out of the old Head of Remedial Department post, or whatever euphemism was employed for it, its progression from the more traditional approaches chronicled by McCall (1980). External support, on the other hand has always lain outside the school's direct organisation: at one point, "advisory teachers" or "peripatetic remedial teachers" had the role of servicing schools in their dealings with pupils with learning problems. For many of them it was only a small step - though one frequently involving considerable expansion of numbers - to categorise themselves as members of a support network. Although the roles of these two forms of supporters may overlap in many ways, it is important to remember that the demands that their jobs place upon them in terms of allegiance, identity and accountability, will make them require differing strengths and capacities.

It is not the intention of this chapter to reiterate the principles of "access" - access to an appropriate curriculum, to specialist expertise, to peer contact - that were embodied in the Warnock Report's (D.E.S., 1978) commendation of the idea of a Special Education Advisory and Support Service which would work alongside support systems within a school. Davis (1980) has done this, and provided models of such provision which reflect those put forward, in one shape or another, by most special needs advisers and embodied in innumerable local education authorities' policy statements. Similarly, authors such as Garnett (1983) have attempted to define the role of those facilitating such access. Campaign plans of this nature are all very well, but flow charts, diagrams, job descriptions and rhetoric often do little to reflect the reality of what actually occurs or what is possible. It is not good enough to define a role, to determine to whom its incumbent is answerable and to exhort such processes as "collaboration", "communication", "innovation" or "attitude change". Davis (1980) has acknowledged the paucity of staff with appropriate experience, training and qualifications to meet the multifarious demands which he outlines; it seems likely, despite the optimistic initiatives detailed by Ivor Ambrose in Chapter 2, that they will remain in short supply for some time to come.

The Special Needs Coordinator

These days it would be a brave or reactionary Head Teacher who dubbed a member of staff "Head of Remedial". We only have to go back to 1982, however, to find Geof Sewell recommending a change of this title to that of "Co-ordinator of Special Education". Sewell (1982) saw the new role primarily in terms of staff training - in the teaching of reading and in working on English across the curriculum in "enhancing the capabilities of teachers in other subject departments with low expectation pupils" (p.59) - but he also specified a specific "support" function. It is unclear, beyond being given additional departmental responsibility for "special needs" resources, quite what such support might consist of in excess of the satisfaction of belonging to a like-minded group. The thoughts of educational writers, though, do not always become translated into practice; we need to look at current jobs to see if Sewell's recommendations have actually bitten.

One way of finding out about what is expected of a role incumbent is to look at the job description. This may not, of course, necessarily reflect what he or she actually does; what it can be assumed to do is to provide an outline of the way in which the employing organisation - in this case the school - conceptualises and proposes to assimilate that role. With this in mind a content analysis of twenty newly-advertised senior special needs posts in Secondary (11-18) or Upper (14-18) schools was conducted in the early part of 1986. Job descriptions can of course be eloquent in their omissions, and this had to be borne in mind; the final sample of twenty was devised after screening out those documents which said little or nothing about the nature of the job.

The post title

The term "co-ordinator" cropped up in the job title only in a quarter of the sample. A further 60 percent were described as "Head" or "Teacher-in-Charge" of special educational needs in the school, reflecting the departmental structures that existed in the school as a whole. This may sound like a minor distinction to make, but the words used to describe a given role are likely also to encapsulate the thinking of those responsible for its creation and maintenance.

"Compensatory education" is a term not often heard these days, implying as it does that its recipients have been subject to some form of earlier deprivation. One post, though, was billed as "Head of Compensatory Studies". One brave soul actually clung firmly to the title "Head of Remedial Education"; in contrast to such a reactionary stance, however, another head teacher had conceived the title "Head of Curriculum Support", reflecting the intention that special needs teachers should "work alongside" teachers in the main school.

Expectations

What, then, was generally expected of the post incumbents and, related to this, at what level in the organisation's hierarchy was responsibility for pupils with special needs placed? Of the twenty schools in the sample, only one post was paid at Scale 2; at the other end of the spectrum, the co-ordinator in one school was a deputy head. Of the rest, seven held Scale 4 posts, and eleven Scale 3. It is worth noting that many of the schools were large enough to warrant senior teacher posts; it is likely, therefore, that even when the teacher with responsibility for special needs was paid at Scale 4, there were at least seven more senior posts within the school.

The term "support" (for other staff members) cropped up in more than half the job descriptions, although an operational definition of this process was hard to find. When one did appear, it placed emphasis upon "working closely" with other heads of department in evaluating and developing the curriculum, helping departments select and produce resources suitable for slow learning children, and liaising with external "support" agencies. What emerged strongly was the need for a role incumbent to possess skills which would enable them to carry out "soft" interventions; in other words, to achieve influence in subject departments without any formal power being designated to them.

What also came across from many of the job descriptions was a tendency to cling to well-tried and probably safer methods of working, even when consultancy and support were mentioned. Although a new orthodoxy now seems to exist in which help in the classroom is seen as particularly desirable, more than half the job descriptions specified some responsibility for organising groups withdrawn from their normal classrooms for additional help, usually in relation to English or Mathematics. Subsequent interviews with job incumbents showed that many teachers retained the expectation that such a service would be performed by the Special Needs Department. For some Department Heads, this was an expectation which had firmly to be squashed; others felt, though, that a rejection of so popular a practice would lead to the alienation of some subject specialist teachers and to a diminution of the Department's influence.

Although analyses of the job descriptions were more exhaustive than can be reported here, of particular relevance to the theme of this chapter were the extent to which staff management and in-service training were seen to fall within the scope of the Special Needs Head. In exactly half the sample, some responsibility for INSET was mentioned, though the extent and nature of any such duties were invariably vaguely couched. Direct staff management responsibility was seldom mentioned: words like "liaise", "consult", "advise" and "support" cropped up far more frequently. It was common to find phrases such as "Heads of Departments and teachers in other subject areas welcome advice from the Head of Special Needs and cooperate fully and gladly." From much of the language, it seemed that those responsible for Special Needs might expect to function in one large, happy corporate family; as I have pointed out elsewhere, however (Bowers, 1984), this is an unlikely state of affairs.

The experience

Job descriptions - particularly those that are published for general consumption - tend to reflect someone other than the job incumbent's view of the post. They provide pictures of the ways in which those with responsibility for providing direction and achieving change think about a given role, and as such they have value. As operational portraits, however, they may prove lacking. To generate further information, twelve of the role occupants themselves were interviewed; a few of the themes which arose are worthy of note in the context of this chapter.

Despite the recent proliferation of one-year full-time courses in special education, or their part-time equivalents, only one person in this sample had actually pursued study of this duration. Five had followed a one-term course of the kind initiated by the D.E.S. and described by Ivor Ambrose in Chapter 2, and a further Special Needs Head had followed a Reading Diploma with the Open University in her own time. Slightly less than half, therefore, had had no formal preparation for their role.

If the qualifications of this group typify those of teachers in similar posts in secondary schools (and a recent survey of one L.E.A. by Taylor (1987) suggests that they do), it would appear that the length of specialist training which they have received does not compare favourably with the preparation of those with similar responsibilities in special schools. In almost all cases, those in leadership positions in special schools will have received at least one year's - or its part-time equivalent - specialist training. Such a discrepancy is probably acceptable where mainstream schools' special needs departments are expected to serve the population identified by the Warnock Committee (D.E.S., 1978) as already in those schools and frequently referred to in administrators' jargon as "the eighteen percent". When, though, moves are suggested (e.g. Booth and Potts, 1983) or recommended (Fish, 1985) which involve the concentration of more severely learning disabled pupils into ordinary schools, we may question whether those at present responsible for decision-making in relation to special needs have been adequately equipped for their task. If the expectations voiced recently by Mittler (1986), that children with complex learning difficulties should increasingly be provided from within ordinary schools, are to be implemented it must surely be necessary to see that those responsible within the organisation for planning and monitoring their educational progress are at least as thoroughly prepared as they would have been in times when special schools were the first placement choice.

Two thirds of the group interviewed had subject teaching responsibilities besides their special needs brief, although the amount of time given to them varied considerably. One devoted just one period to other tasks, while another gave as many as ten to specific subject work. Only four spent a significant proportion of their time in supporting other teachers; four more devoted between two and six periods to assistance within other classes, whilst the remaining four worked in schools where such activity did not occur.

What emerges from this limited sample is a fairly fragmented profile of heads of special needs in secondary schools, in terms of internal status, preparation and role responsibilities. The school cannot operate in isolation, and a well developed special needs service within a secondary school must surely take account of such related issues as the curriculum of feeder schools, the monitoring of learning problems of those likely to enter the school, advising parents on ways in which they can assist their child's learning, and the work of other agencies concerned with children's welfare. Of the twelve, however, only five had any contact with feeder schools, and one of these attributed this not to a special needs role but to their status as head of their school's Lower School. Of these five, two only made one brief visit to each contributing school every year. Just half the group sampled had any contact at all with parents, and responses to subsequent questioning on their purpose and the techniques employed suggested that only two involved parents in any defined way: both were concerned with assisting and encouraging paired reading at home. All had some contact with external agencies, particularly the School Psychological Service; it was surprising, though, that of these twelve coordinators, three said that they had more than a little to do with outside professionals.

Probably the feature which most characterised the secondary coordinator's role in this sample was the responsibility for testing pupils. In all but one case, coordinators had responsibility for ensuring that various attainment and aptitude tests were administered to all first year pupils; their duties included interpreting results which were linked to intervention decisions. The rationale for such testing lay in the need to gain "objective" comparisons of children's performance in such areas as vocabulary, the comprehension of written material, the computational and problem-solving abilities in mathematics. The exception was only one of administration: the English Department controlled the school's entry testing. It seems ironic that at a time when educational psychologists - whose discipline and subsequent training include an understanding of the strengths and limitations of tests - are eschewing psychometrics (cf. Gillham, 1978; Quicke, 1982), schools are placing increasing emphasis upon testing to screen, set and select pupils as part of their internal categorisation. Many reported that they felt inadequately prepared for this particular role, particularly when questioned on what qualities they might look for in selecting tests and what criteria they would employ in defining cut-off scores on the instruments used. The duty to test usually was defined by senior management in the schools, the assumption being made that the special needs coordinator was the appropriate person to carry out this function. Despite attempts to reform assessment at eleven-plus, it seems that testing remains with us as part of the internal process of selection within many secondary schools. If it has to be done, it is far better that the administration and interpretation of tests should be carried out by competent and informed personnel; this brief survey, though, strongly suggested that very few of those interviewed had achieved this state.

What was also revealed by the follow-up interviews was a tendency of the special needs coordinators to experience what might be termed "job isolation". Many of them felt that their concerns were not those of their colleagues and that they were in some way performing a different function from those of other heads of departments. We might expect this to be reduced by a school approach which encouraged the retention of pupils with learning difficulties within their ordinary classes, allowing the special needs specialist to work alongside subject colleagues. However, whilst this was seen by some respondents to reduce the sense of separateness, it went only part of the way to achieving this; they still differed from the subject specialists in that they worked in somebody else's classroom with somebody else's pupils. Their role was one of servicing others' teaching and this itself generated a sense of separateness.

How can we explain the apparent paradox of a collaborating member of staff still feeling isolated? Surely if they operate as an integrated team member within a "whole-school approach" to special needs, they will lose any feelings of exclusivity. Payne (1982) has identified a number of different forms of specialisation within teams, each contributing to some sense of exclusion from the concerns of other members: "domain specialisation", where the client group is the basis of specialisation; "task specialisation", where skills and activities are specialised; and "role specialisation" where a particular position is occupied in the team. A special needs coordinator is likely to experience all three and, as Payne remarks, "Specialisation is strongest where all three of these go together" (p.91). Solutions to the reported isolation, if required at all, are not easy to come by. Traditional remedies are the complete sharing of expertise (Payne, 1982), and it might make sense for the specialist to work towards this end. Realistically, however, this is probably impractical in most schools, particularly as the intake of children with more severe learning difficulties in such areas as speech and language, motor impairment or emotional disorders makes greater, not less specialism essential.

Internal and external support

So far, we have looked particularly at people supporting special needs pupils and their teachers who are themselves part of the school's staff. "Support" has always been with us: the act of removing a child to a segregated remedial department or withdrawing that child from his or her lessons for additional coaching in English or Mathematics was usually justified because the child needed additional help or because the child's teacher required assistance. The meaning of the word, within a special educational context, has simply changed.

With the calling into question of the whole notion of "remedial" education, the view of support that accompanied it had inevitably to change. The term "remedial", with its medical connotations, suggests that there is something wrong with the child that requires a remedy. It is the child who is at fault, whilst the school has no need to review its own methods or practice. The suitability of this perspective is now being increasingly challenged; we are becoming more accustomed to looking at a child in its context and to questioning the relevance of the curriculum and the styles with which it is delivered. Nowhere is this more evident than in the field of behaviour disorders (e.g. Gillham, 1981; Tattum, 1986), where the idea that a child should fit in or get out has been variously challenged by a wide range of authors.

With this modification in the attitude at least of those making decisions at L.E.A. level, just who is now being supported? A recent N.F.E.R. survey (Hegarty et al, in press) of external support services sees a change towards the teacher rather than the pupil being the client: the support teacher now becomes a consultant, providing a service to the teacher in the classroom in modifying teaching approaches and materials, and to the school as a whole in reviewing the ways in which learning and behaviour problems are dealt with. The model adopted corresponds to that which is increasingly favoured by educational psychologists (Burden, 1981; Quicke, 1982): it holds firstly that many pupils described as problems or problematical by those in authority in schools can usefully be viewed as problems of the schools themselves rather than of individuals or of society at large. Secondly, an effective consultant must understand how both the explicit and implicit organisational structures of a school influence pupils' attitudes and performance. Thirdly, the model contends that schools can be viewed as open systems: any change within the school or outside it will potentially influence all other aspects of the school. So, for example, the closure of a nearby special school will have an obvious impact on the demands made on the special needs resources of the ordinary school; so also will a change in pastoral care policy, or even a change in a teacher in one subject department, potentially influence the process and practice of the special needs service in a school. This phenomenon has recently been expressed in a general context by Hartley and Kelly (1986) who point out that "Psychologists have come to appreciate the systemic character of organisations, and the ways in which small-scale organisational change can have a variety of effects across interdependent organisation sub-systems" (p.169). To the consultancy role, then, can be added that of "systems interventionist" (Burden, 1981); put more simply, the supporter has also to be a doer and changer.

Boundary issues

The special needs supporter may operate "in-house", as part of the staff of a school or, like the educational psychologist, may be part of an infrastructure of external services. Despite their similarity of focus, it is obvious that the two jobs will differ quite significantly. For one, of course, the major concern will be a single school, whilst for the other that school will be just part of a wider caseload. But the differences go further than that. We can liken the first to a denisen of a country who may visit other regions of that nation, who may have to adjust to some differences in culture, but whose allegiances and identity are broadly similar to those of the people whom he or she encounters. Boundaries have to be crossed, but they are only provincial boundaries. In contrast, the external supporter is like a traveller abroad, who crosses national boundaries and must learn to adapt to languages and cultures which may be quite different from his or her own.

Distinguishing between "in-school" and "itinerant" support teachers, Topping (1983) has observed that the latter, whilst disadvantaged by not knowing schools intimately, have the advantage of a resultant increase in objectivity. The idea of "objectivity", however, is highly questionable. What it means is that the "objective" individual's perspective differs from that of the "subjective" person. Their own "objective" view is likely to be coloured and distorted by their organisational and professional culture; the potential weakness, therefore, of the external support agent is the assumption of objectivity. If the teachers in a school form his or her client group, it is first necessary to understand their assumptions about pupil failure or noncompliance, to appreciate their emotional responses to such behaviour and to accept that their present solutions and suggestions, however dysfunctional they may appear to be, provide their best available coping mechanisms. The judgemental consultant, who knows better than his or her clients, has much in common with Victorian missionaries in Africa who sought change in others through an assumption of their own rectitude and cultural superiority.

From this, it sounds as though the external supporter needs a range of client-centred counselling skills (Rogers, 1951; Egan, 1975), and some L.E.A.s have committed inservice resources to counselling training for their support workers. Such steps are to be welcomed, but they are probably not enough. A support teacher has to be more than a counsellor and more than a skilled teacher of children with special needs. He or she has to be a catalyst, a change agent, and as such needs - whether in-school or externally based - the skills of a consultant. Of course, consultants have been around for years in special education, and ordinary schools have had considerable dealings with them in the shape of educational psychologists and others. If support teachers are to avoid many of the difficulties of boundary demarcation and communication which Johnson (1980) has chronicled in relation to comprehensive schools, it is important that they should look closely at what is involved in the consultant role.

Supporters as consultants

In education, we frequently accept proficiency in one job as a qualification to do another for which the individual has no record of success. Thus head teachers are recruited from the ranks of successful teachers, although their management experience may be negligible; similarly, lecturers in education have been concerned with service delivery in one form or another, yet the skills which their new job calls for may differ considerably from those which they have so far shown. In just the same way, we now expect those who have a proven track record in teaching children with special needs to transfer easily to acting in a supportive role to other teachers, and to be able to modify their child-related skills to their consultative position.

As Dessent (1984) has observed, the satisfactions which a teacher derives from face-to-face contact with children may be absent in an advisory role. The skills which he or she developed may become largely redundant when the objects of intervention - the child and the way it is taught - are severed by at least one stage, and new skills may have to be acquired.

Consultancy

This is a very fashionable term. We have only to survey the Situations Vacant columns of the more up-market newspapers to see a succession of jobs for "financial consultants", "software consultants", "management consultants" and their ilk. It is also a term which applies increasingly to those offering "outreach" services to schools, as Maggie Balshaw's chapter in this book emphasises. Interestingly, at a time when the medical model of childhood disabilities has lost favour in special education, the term "consultant" has probably greatest status and is more time-honoured in the medical profession than in any other. What, though, does consultancy entail?

Egan (1978) has presented a model of consultancy which involves three roles: the consultant attempts to influence a target via the efforts of a mediator. So, in our terms, the teacher consultant will work through one or more teachers or other staff to change the academic performance or behaviour of pupils within the school. The consultant does not deal directly with the target, although he or she may observe the interactions between mediator and target. The skills which he sees the consultant possessing are those of:

(i) **Diagnosis.** This does not mean diagnosing learning difficulties: rather it entails assessing the readiness and capability of individuals or an organisation to change the ways in which they operate.

(ii) **Producing new perspectives.** The consultant must be able to help the mediator to see new possibilities - new ways of organising learning, new ways of dealing with a problem pupil - which the mediator can relate to and feel responsible for.

(iii) **Goal setting.** The consultant shows the mediator how to go about establishing priorities and setting behavioural goals.

(iv) **Choosing means.** Whatever goals are set, a way to achieve them must be established. Here the consultant must assist in establishing what responses need to be made available and what changes in structure should be brought about.   Where a child is inattentive and off-task, for example, it is not sufficient for a teacher to define the goals of intermittent reinforcement of attention to task and reduced time-span demands for given pieces of work;   such changes may require a different way of the teacher organising not only what he or she does but what the rest of the class do as well.

(v) **Programme implementation.** Here the consultant needs to provide feedback to the mediator on initial progress and to make that person, or the organisation as a whole, more aware of the sources of subsequent feedback through which to monitor success.

(vi) **Programme evaluation.** Here the consultant shows the mediator how to make evaluation a constructive on-going process within the system, rather than a judgemental final statement.

For Egan (1978) then, a consultant has to be an educator, trainer, observer, monitor and supervisor. However, as has already been touched upon, there are differences between the processes of internal consultancy and external consultancy. In what ways may we expect these differences to influence the work of school-based special needs staff and external special needs support staff?

Internal consultants

There are a number of issues involved in internal consultancy of which the school-centred special needs support teacher needs to be aware. Whilst some of them may appear obvious, it is easy to ignore them when embroiled in the job. A survey of the literature on consultancy suggests that they include:

(i) Learning how to play by the school's rules. These are not the formal or informal rules which apply to pupils, but the unwritten and frequently unspoken ways of doing things which exist in any organisation. It involves knowing who has the power to enable things to be done (c.f. Bowers, 1984), and knowing what latent conflict to avoid arousing.

(ii) Achieving autonomy. Since the internal consultant is a member of the organisation's staff, it is important that he or she should clearly establish with senior management the extent to which they are able to choose with whom and how they want to work. Without such autonomy, the consultant's role is likely to become shaped by others' views of it; for example, one special needs coordinator in a comprehensive school found herself instructed by the Head of English on which pupils she was to teach when she provided support within his department's lessons, how many she should deal with at a time, and what she should teach them. Without asserting her own view of her role, she was quickly reduced to an auxiliary helper.

(iii) Building individuality through successful work and viable projects: being seen to be effective by one's colleagues.

(iv) Developing relationships and trust over a period of time.

(v) Staying politically free: not taking sides or getting "dragged into" other people's disputes even though they may appear to be linked with one's own concerns.

(vi) Managing multiple masters and agendas. The internal special needs consultant may see him or herself as being accountable to a variety of individuals. One of these will probably be the head teacher, but others may be educational psychologists, educational advisers or inspectors, and possibly external support teachers responsible for a number of schools. There will be times when the priorities and expectations of these people will conflict and it is only too easy for the internal consultant to become enmeshed in disputes over what is best for individual pupils or the development of the school or education service as a whole.

(vii) Gaining client-group commitment to the projects with which the consultant is involved; in other words, getting more than grudging acceptance from other teachers that the support teacher's aims and values are their own as well.

Although many of the skills, much of the knowledge and several of the personal attributes which are required of the internal consultant are also necessary for successful external consultancy, there are also differences in the demands of the two jobs. One "belongs" to the organisation in which his or her clients are central, while the other, however hard he or she may try to appear to do so, does not. Among the differing issues with which the external consultant is faced, are:

(i) The management of "role potency"; in other words, the external support teacher must be able to create an acceptance that he or she has something important to offer and is a significant member of the wider organisation: the local education authority. Some educational psychologists, despite their prestigious title, have experienced difficulties in this area. Support teachers must ensure that they are not seen as pale imitations of the visiting educational psychologist.

(ii) Taking on short-term projects. In many cases, the external consultant will be called in over specific issues, rather than participating in an on-going colleague relationship. He or she must know how to start a project and, when the time is right, how to withdraw.

(iii) Coping with variety. For the school-based teacher there is a degree of reassuring routine attached to the school day. This may at times be humdrum, but it also creates a framework within which days and weeks can be organised. The external support consultant may find that no two days are the same, that one week is not necessarily like the one before, and that new people have to be met and related to with unpredictable frequency.

(iv) Linked with variety, of course, are the demanding pace and pressures which the external support teacher is likely to encounter. There will be travelling time to take into account in much of his or her work; arriving late and flustered from a traffic jam can reduce effective performance, particularly where there is pressure to be seen to be effective. Clients are likely to make demands on the supporter's time, and expect that those demands are met; colleagues may expect advice or in-service training assistance at the drop of a hat; criticism may come if the consultant is not seen to be readily accessible and available.

(v) There will also be the stress of ambiguity. Inevitably the external supporter's environment is a less predictable and familiar one than the internal support teacher's own school.

(vi) Coping with cultural shock: consulting with a variety of clients, quickly appraising situations and assimilating the norms, politics and relationships within many different schools and other organisations, such as the L.E.A. Advisory Service and School Psychological Service.

(vii) Dealing with loneliness. Independent work and travel inevitably means that the individual is frequently cast upon his or her own resources. Even though working in schools, the consultant can - and should - never truly belong to the organisation. This is of course a phenomenon to which peripatetic teachers have long been accustomed; it can be alleviated to some extent by having a strong home-based team of which the consultant is a member and to which he or she can refer anxieties, concerns and difficulties. However, there is a danger that such a team may develop its own norms, politics and culture in such a way as to render entry into schools and acceptance by their staff more difficult for the consultant.

Selling a Service

There is one characteristic of the consultant which both internal and external special needs support teachers are likely to require. Within the caring professions generally it is unfashionable, and for some even abhorrent, to look at commercial practices in developing models for service delivery. But the Health Services have had to adjust reluctantly to the recommendations of the Griffiths Report and the establishment of General and Unit Managers; similarly, I have pointed out (Bowers, 1984a) that special educational provision is likely to be judged increasingly in terms of its cost-effectiveness. Good consultants "sell" their services; they convince others that they have something worthwhile to offer. Their success may be measured by the benefits which accrue to their clients (in our case teachers and **their** clients, the children), but however good their interventions may be, they will never have the chance

95

to take effect if they are not accepted as worth trying in the first place.

The effective support consultant, then, has to be able to promote his or her services. This has for some time been recognised by psychologists. Tizard (1976) has remarked ". . . we have not convinced the public that we are a really important profession" (p.230). Extending this, Cullen and Wright (1978) have argued that the work of professional psychologists has much to benefit from a study of successful sales techniques; to this end they reframe sales training literature in more familiar behavioural terms. The idea of "selling", of course, has uncomfortable commercial connotations for many "people-centred" professionals. However, if we look at selling as seeking to influence specific areas of other individuals' behaviour, we can see that this is what any interventionist in schools - whether they work directly with children or with teachers, as the support consultant is likely to do - is endeavouring to achieve.

The critical skills of selling

As we have seen, the job of the support consultant calls for competencies and qualities which may require the successful classroom teacher considerably to extend his or her repertoire. Whilst all aspects of selling psychology are not necessarily relevant to this changed role, it is worth looking at what characteristics distinguish between successful and unsuccessful salespeople, at the same time considering what applications these may have to this growing area of special educational activity.

In an extensive study involving critical incident technique, Kirchner and Dunnette (1957) found fifteen different categories which distinguished between effective and ineffective sales personnel. Using similar methods, Poppleton and Lubbock (1977) distinguished eleven characteristics which were indicative of success. The important ones from the point of view of this chapter are the following:

(i) **Showing and generating enthusiasm for the product.**
In our case, the "product" can be seen in two terms - the necessary development of the child or children whose special needs the teacher must attempt to meet, and the kinds of curricular or organisational approaches which are envisaged. If the support teacher doesn't show a belief in the importance and effectiveness of what he or she is doing, then it is unlikely that clients will do so either.

(ii) **Paying attention to the customer's needs, feelings and requirements.** As we have discussed earlier, the

96

"customer" is likely to be a single teacher, or perhaps a group of teachers constituting a secondary school department or the staff of a primary school. To enable change, it is first necessary for the support consultant really to listen and to appreciate the concerns and expectations of his or her clients.

(iii) **Showing integrity and professionalism.** This means giving accurate information, not holding back relevant facts and opinions, carrying out promises, respecting confidences, and the many other facets of behaviour which generate confidence in a person's honesty and trustworthiness.

(iv) **Planning and organising.** Knowing what a visit is about; doing one's homework beforehand (e.g. finding out about a child's past difficulties, discussing with colleagues the merits of materials which may be recommended); keeping records of each call to a classroom or a school and not relying on memory.

(v) **Working steadily with relatively little supervision.** Here the ability to self-motivate and self-minister is very important.

(vi) **Devoting time and energy to work activities over and above the minimum requirements.** For the support consultant, this may involve such things as seeing all clients regularly, finding out about new learning materials which become available, attending INSET activities, persisting with awkward or apathetic teacher clients, or even reading books on education!

(vii) **Making effective contacts with prospective customers.** It isn't enough to wait for them to come to you. Go out and let people know you are there and what you can offer; join appropriate specialist organisations, and local working parties; be prepared to help initially in a variety of ways which may not typify the way in which you expect to work later.

(viii) **Showing mood control.** Remaining calm when others become emotionally involved, excited, or show signs of stress. The support consultant may sometimes have to deal with people at times of crisis, when his or her clients are not coping well. It is important to maintain as level a mood as possible, and not to be either "sucked in" to others' heightened emotions or to respond antagonistically to them.

Some other key points arise from a survey of successful

97

selling practice which may be relevant to those organising a support service. There is a considerable amount of evidence (e.g. Vernon, 1964) that people tend to like others who in a variety of ways are similar to themselves. It is important to consider this in ascribing support staff to particular individuals or schools; where a team is operating, it is probably best that members should be matched as far as possible to their clients on variables which include age, sex, style of dress and attitude to authority.

A critical social skill in selling, and likely to be contributory to effective consultancy, is the handling of objections: in other words, the other person's reasons for not wanting to accept what the proposer has to offer. Successful sales people have been shown (Poppleton, 1981) to listen to objections without interruption rather than rebutting them without hearing them in full. They show the other person that they understand them and take them seriously. They are also unlikely to get into a lengthy argument over any particular objection. These character-istics should be borne in mind by the zealous consultant who may be so committed to what he or she wants to happen that they are prepared to argue vehemently for it.

In conclusion

It is quite apparent that we are seeing a movement away from special needs specialists working directly with children. As pressure for mainstreaming of handicapped children increases and as schools attempt to develop a "whole school" approach, the case for separate educational provi-sion, even within the confines of the ordinary school, becomes less easy to sustain.

Support for the ordinary teacher, whether in the form of an internal specialist or an externally-based or "itinerant" colleague, is a model which has proliferated and is likely to go on doing so in the near future. What we have to do, in deciding on who should do such a job and how they should be equipped, is to consider whether the demonstration of adequate child-related teaching skills is enough. It is the contention of this chapter that it is not. The effective support teacher will need competencies in adult human relationships which can be placed under the broad umbrella of "consultancy skills". This new professional is going increasingly to be called upon to operate in an arena which until recently has been strange to those working with special needs pupils. It is essential that he or she should be adequately attired before stepping into the open.

Chapter Six

BRINGING THE SPECIAL NEEDS DEPARTMENT OUT OF THE CUPBOARD

Martyn Rouse

Introduction

One of the most significant developments in special
needs provision in ordinary schools over the last decade has
been the way in which remedial teachers have been developing
their roles to include support for their colleagues. There
has been an increasing awareness that effective whole school
responses to special educational needs will only be achieved
if all teachers accept responsibility for a wider range of
needs in their classrooms. It is suggested that many
teachers will need support to enable them to do this
successfully.

In this chapter I intend to consider some of the issues
which arise when working in support of one's colleagues and
to suggest some approaches which might enable such support to
be more effective. The ideas are developed from my own
former work, both as head of a remedial department and an
advisory teacher.

Overview

The pressure for reform and development of secondary special
needs provision takes places at a time when schools are
facing increasing demands from a variety of sources and
initiatives. Any debate about the future role of special
needs departments must take place within the context of the
changing climate in which schools exist today.

Questions about the most appropriate form of provision
for children with learning difficulties are not new and have
been debated for decades. The mid-nineteen seventies saw a
widespread questioning of some of the arrangements primary
and secondary schools were making at that time to cope with
such children. The two most common arrangements were special
classes and withdrawal (remedial) groups.

Special classes were becoming less popular for a number

of reasons. They had the disadvantage that they often became 'sinks' of low teacher expectation and poor pupil self concept. The techniques and processes used in selecting children for such groups were of questionable reliability. Usually what was taught in such classes bore little relationship to what was going on elsewhere in the school. Consequently children suffered from 'curriculum distancing', a potentially chronic condition which meant that it became progressively more difficult to transfer pupils back into the mainstream of the school. It was common for teachers and pupils in such groups to feel that they were not a real part of the school. For many children placed in special classes the only escape from the sink was down the educational plug-hole of disaffection and truancy.

Remedial (withdrawal) groups largely replaced special classes (McCall, 1980; Clunies-Ross and Wimhurst 1983) and often led to short-term improvement in pupils' performance, particularly in reading. However, this progress was not usually reflected in other areas of the curriculum. Some subject specialist colleagues would still complain about 'the remedials' being unable to cope with the demands of their subjects, and pupils often resented being taken out of subjects or groups they liked to be given extra reading and language work. Sadly, in most schools it was rare to find that what was being done in remedial classes related to other class work.

It was shown a long time ago by such workers as Chazan (1967), Cashdan and Pumfrey (1969) and Lovell et al (1962, 1963) that even spectacular gains brought about by withdrawing pupils for remedial help tended to be only short-lived and resulted in little long-term benefit. It was thought that by concentrating on literacy, and to a lesser extent numeracy, remedial teachers were not helping children with learning difficulties to take advantage of the wider curriculum schools had on offer. Reporting on a number of visits to secondary schools, H.M.I. reported:

> "In many cases remedial teachers, conscious of the school's expectation that they should succeed in a clearly defined task, had restricted the range and character of what they offered to exclude all but what they considered basic essentials. Often this restriction led to impoverishment" (D.E.S., 1984, p.15).

In many remedial departments, much of the work only concentrated on the pupil's weaknesses and ignored whatever strengths the pupils may have possessed.

Whose Responsibility?

It may even have been the presence of a remedial department, staffed by 'experts' in learning difficulties, who always taught 'failing' pupils in small groups, which reinforced the message that such pupils were not the responsibility of subject teachers. It was not uncommon to hear subject specialist colleagues arguing that if some pupils were seen to need small group teaching by 'experts' for part of the time, how could they as teachers of their subjects to groups of 30 be expected to cope with them in their classes?

The dilemma was that at a time when some subject specialist teachers were requesting more withdrawal of failing pupils, many remedial teachers were questioning some of the assumptions upon which remedial provision was based. This in turn led to a debate about how schools might meet children's special educational needs more effectively. The National Association for Remedial Education (N.A.R.E.) organised two conferences in 1975 and 1977 to consider the future of remedial education. One result of this debate was the call for remedial teachers to widen their role by broadening the concept of remedial education to ensure that children in receipt of remedial education were not deprived of valuable aspects of the curriculum (Gains and McNicolas, 1978). A number of attempts have been made to define the role of remedial teachers in the light of the debate about the effectiveness of what they were doing (e.g. Bailey, 1981; Laskier, 1985; O'Hagen, 1977 and Bines, 1986).

The Warnock Report (D.E.S., 1978) and the Education Act (D.E.S., 1981) both stress the need for remedial teachers to adopt a wider special needs role. A possible framework for this development is described in Teaching Roles for Special Educational Needs (N.A.R.E., 1985). Seven roles for the special needs coordinator in the future are envisaged:-

1. An assessment role
2. A prescriptive role
3. A teaching/pastoral role
4. A supportive role
5. A liaison role
6. A management role
7. A staff development role.

I now propose to look in more detail at number four, the suggested supportive role, in the light of my own experiences as we, in our school, made our first moves to work in this way.

Support: The Background

In September 1980, acknowledging this debate and in response to feelings of dissatisfaction about existing provision, a small scale experiment was set up in a North London Comprehensive School at which I was then Head of the Remedial Department. The scheme intended to provide support across the curriculum in an attempt to give children with learning difficulties greater access to what the school had to offer. More than forty periods each week of remedial teachers' time was allocated to supporting subject specialist colleagues. Whilst it was realised that support could be provided without going into lessons by helping with the preparation and adaptation of appropriate materials, we took our lead from Gulliford (1979) who noted that, (p.149):

"the development of remedial work across the curriculum in secondary schools requires a partnership between subject specialists and remedial teachers."

What closer partnership could there be than the remedial teacher and the subject specialist teacher sharing their own expertise to the process of helping the child with learning difficulties to be more successful?

As is common with many educational initiatives, insufficient time was available to plan exactly how the remedial teacher would work in support. Members of the remedial department felt that it was important that we should, where possible, join our subject colleagues in their classrooms and laboratories. We were unsure about whether it would be best to concentrate our activities on those pupils with the most acute learning difficulties by sitting them together with the remedial teacher: the disadvantages of creating a remedial group 'in situ' were apparent. As there was nowhere to turn to for guidance on these points, it was decided that flexibility was essential. We hoped that the best arrangements would develop once the scheme was in operation.

Even at that early stage, before a start had been made, it was clear that there would be changes as the professional relationship between the two teachers developed. To allow for this, an element of evaluation and subsequent modification was incorporated. This was to be through regular meetings of the partners in order to discuss, prepare, criticise and reject what was proving to be of little value and to add what seemed promising.

The scheme was embarked upon with open minds, with no one really knowing what to expect.

The Scheme in Operation

At the beginning of the scheme, three remedial teachers and eight subject specialists were involved. This amounted to a total of 42 periods a week in which classes would be co-taught.

It was clear from quite an early stage that not all 'teams' were working as successfully as others. By the end of the scheme's first year, about one-fifth of the arrangements had changed to such an extent that these teachers could no longer be described as teaching together. In most of these 'failed' cases, the remedial teacher had begun withdrawing some pupils for a separate session in the subject concerned. This was particularly disappointing because we had not set out to extend withdrawal groups across the curriculum. Such a situation ran counter to the whole rationale of the scheme.

The reasons why some of these 'teams' had failed to work together were not immediately obvious. In some cases teachers from 'failed teams' appeared to be working success fully with other colleagues. A possible explanation was perhaps something to do with the relationship which developed between the two teachers concerned. It later became clear that a crucial element in such a scheme concerns the inter-action of the people involved and how they see their respective roles in such an arrangement.

A search of the literature at the time in an attempt to find possible explanations for some of the 'failed' teams proved fruitless. Hargreaves (1972) has noted that in spite of extensive research into teacher-pupil relations and pupil-teacher relations, there has been almost no systematic research into teacher-teacher relationships. Even during the period of rapid growth in the popularity of team-teaching in primary schools, there were few accounts of teachers finding it difficult to work together. There is little doubt that there were failures at this time. However, reporting such matters is difficult because of ethical and professional considerations. Intrusion into the privacy of the classroom is often resented. Such factors have always meant that matters relevant to the teacher's classroom role are very delicate and difficult to pin down.

Morrison and McIntyre (1969) point out:

> "Where teachers are working together both in planning and in actual teaching, conflict between them becomes more likely and more damaging in its consequences. If two members of staff differ widely in their educational attitudes and goals, they are unlikely to be able to cooperate closely."

One of the reasons why such warnings are often ignored in the planning stage of such schemes may have something to do with the enthusiasm and energy with which they are launched. More recently Thomas (1986) notes that,

> "Despite moves to team teaching some years ago, despite the prevalence of more than one person in the special school classroom . . . . there has been little research undertaken into the effective use of more than one adult in the classroom. Such a situation contrasts sharply with the position in industry where simultaneous problems and opportunities created when more than one person get together on a task are confronted by an enormous management literature" (p.19).

With the benefit of hindsight, it now seems naive that we could have embarked upon such a potentially major change in the way teachers are expected to work without reflecting upon some of the interpersonal and management issues which are an inevitable part of such developments. To be effective in developing whole school responses to special educational needs, support teachers will have to leave behind their traditional but narrow roles in which they only taught small groups of failing children, to become consultants on the learning process and agents of change attempting to develop classrooms in which children who are experiencing difficulties can learn more effectively (Hodgson, 1984).

Stages in the Process of Working in Support

Before attempting to work in a support role it may be useful to have a clear picture of the nature of consultancy (cf. Davies, 1977). The stages can be summarised as follows:

1. Gaining entry

This is concerned with building relationships and identifying and establishing the need for support. Good working relationships are essential. Support is more likely to be accepted if subject specialist colleagues are aware that there are children with learning difficulties in their classes who can be helped. Even though the support teacher will be known to his or her colleagues, it is interpersonal skills rather than technical skills and knowledge which are most important at this stage. Without a high degree of commitment and cooperation it is unlikely that much will be achieved. Trust and confidence need to be developed. Teachers are unlikely to take risks for people they do not trust. It must be made clear that what goes on in the class-room will be confidential. A support teacher should not be seen as a spy intent on finding out what goes on in other people's classrooms.

2. Contract formulation

An initial meeting should be held at which the issues concerning roles and responsibilities within the classroom can be discussed. In my opinion it was a lack of clarity about role definition which led to the problems which ulti-mately destroyed some of our co-teaching arrangements. This difficulty with role definition was also commented upon by Ferguson and Adams (1982) when reporting on the Grampian team teaching experiment.

Ideally, both parties should be clear about what this initial meeting is meant to achieve, with clear objectives being laid out. Any differences in expectations should be resolved at this point and any constraints of time or scope should be agreed upon. Discussion should focus on what the support teacher is going to do. Are preparation, presenta-tion and marking to be shared? Who is to be supported - the teacher or the pupils? (It may be necessary to be rather vague on this point.) It can sound rather threatening, even arrogant, to suggest that the support is about to attempt to change the classroom practice of experienced colleagues. A mutually agreed agenda which can reflect the concerns of the teacher will minimise the level of suspicion and any feelings that the support teacher is about to impose solutions whatever the teacher's feelings.

Another effect of such an agreed contract, is that it builds commitment from the teacher, which in turn makes a satisfactory outcome more likely. The recent work of Thomas (1986) provides some useful pointers to these issues.

3. Investigating the situation

Consideration needs to be given to the physical layout of the classsroom and organisation of lessons. Some styles of teaching make support difficult, particularly traditional approaches in which typically the teacher introduces the topic and then pupils do some written work. If this takes place in a formal classroom with the desks in rows and the pupils are not supposed to talk it makes the role of a support teacher almost impossible. We found that science lessons, which tend to be activity-based, with pupil movement around the laboratory, were easier in which to work. The relatively open atmosphere of the laboratory may also have something to do with science teachers' familiarity with sharing their classrooms with laboratory technicians. Another adult in the room was nothing new for them.

It is important at this stage to find out what, if any, arrangements are already being made to accommodate children who may have difficulties. It is easy to undo what progress may have already been made by insensitive intervention. Support teachers need to avoid 'deskilling' their colleagues by imposing solutions where problems either do not exist or are already being solved.

4. Planning the support

Once the support teacher is in possession of sufficient information about the sessions in which they are to work then strategies and tactics can be agreed. Again time needs to be found to discuss these points with colleagues (cf. Lieberman, 1986) because effective collaboration needs to be planned.

The actual style of the intervention is crucial and familiarity with some of the alternatives is a prerequisite of this. The work of Heron (1975) is extremely useful in illuminating this complex area. He suggests that the term 'intervention' is not entirely fortunate as it carries with it connotations of interference. This must be avoided at all costs by having a clear and voluntary contract between supporter and supported in which the main aim is to provide an enabling service and skill to the subject specialist teacher.

Heron recognises six categories of intervention and it may be useful briefly to define them. He groups them under the two headings 'authoritative' and 'facilitative'.

Authoritative

(i) Prescriptive: Giving advice, being judgemental/ critical/evaluative. A prescriptive intervention is one that explicitly seeks to direct the behaviour of the class teacher.

(ii) Informative: Being didactic, informing, instructing and interpreting. An informative intervention seeks to impart new knowledge and information.

(iii) Confronting: Being challenging of restrictive attitudes, beliefs or behaviour. It is unlikely, however, that a subject teacher who has such beliefs will have sought support in the first place.

Facilitative

(iv) Cathartic: Releasing tensions, encouraging laughter and emotional outbursts. Again, this is unlikely to be a useful style of intervention given the constraints of classrooms. It is a style which fits more comfortably in the field of counselling.

(v) Catalytic: Being reflective, encouraging self-directed problem solving. A catalytic intervention seeks to enable the teacher to come up with their own solutions to the problems within their classrooms.

(vi) Supportive: Being approving, confirming and validating. A supportive intervention affirms the worth and value of the teacher.

The first three are described as authoritative since in each case the support teacher would take a more dominant or assertive role. The second set, referred to as facilitative interventions, are more discreet. The support teacher is less obtrusive in directing the subject teacher's behaviour.

It should be pointed out that there is no 'best style' of intervention. None is more significant or important than any other. However, within the constraints of working in classrooms and given that most support will be offered by insiders to the organisation I would suggest that confronting one's colleagues or attempting to work in a cathartic style may be inappropriate. Such styles of working are likely to be more difficult to carry out.

Selecting the most appropriate style will depend upon the information gained. All classrooms are different but a useful rule of thumb would be to start with supportive or catalytic styles on the assumption that colleagues have the solutions to many of their difficulties within them and facilitative intervention will enable them to come up with their own answers. This has the advantage of giving the 'ownership' of the solutions to the class teacher. Having said that, there will be occasions when more prescriptive or informative styles are necessary. Support teachers should, however, avoid the temptation to rush into such authoritative intervention styles in an attempt to demonstrate their technical competence. It is quite likely that the subject teacher will feel undermined if the support teacher is making a series of helpful suggestions and recommendations which they could, with or without the help, have determined for themselves. Heron refers to this creation of dependency as 'benevolent takeover'.

A skill which support teachers will need to develop is the ability to select appropriate intervention and be able to move comfortably from one style to another as the situation in which they are working develops.

5. Action!

The strategies should be implemented. Support should be

provided and progress should be monitored. Regular meetings between team members are essential throughout this, the longest stage. Formative evaluation can constantly be used to amend and develop the chosen ways of working. In our experience it was the regular meetings which provided the opportunity and scope for much of the development of appropriate objectives, materials and methods to help children with learning difficulties. Whilst it is acknowledged that time is at a premium during the teaching day there are ways of enabling special needs teachers and subject departments to work more closely together. The designation of a link or liaison teacher within different subject departments can help with this. In our scheme one of the remedial department teachers moved his 'base' into one of the science preparation rooms so that he could be part of the informal, but essential, discussions which take place between lessons.

The actual roles that the support teacher should take during lessons will depend upon a number of factors. However, it is clear that as a result of our findings and those of Ferguson and Adams (1982) the success of such initiatives depends largely upon how much the support teacher is allowed to feel part of the team. We found it extremely useful for a number of reasons to be involved in the sharing of preparation, presentation and all those other tasks such as marking, report writing and attending parents' evenings. Not to be part of such activities could lead to feelings of resentment on the part of the subject teachers and boredom by support teachers perhaps dissatisfied by their undemanding role.

6. Evaluation and withdrawal

Although it is essential that evaluation should be seen as a continuous process, it should also be noted that such co-teaching arrangements need to come to an end and this should be followed by a debate about outcomes compared with goals. There may have been unexpected benefits. We found more practical science was taking place, a subject teacher admitted that her lessons were better prepared when the support teacher was to be present, there was greater continuity in the case of staff absence, a decrease in the number of sanctions used by one teacher was noted, and there was the chance for special needs teachers to see some of their pupils against a different educational backcloth. The unexpected benefits which were derived from working in this way should not be discounted, but perhaps there are greater prizes to be won.

The Management of Change

The time is probably ripe in some schools for us to move on from considerations of who should be supported and the most effective ways of doing this, to an investigation of the more fundamental issue of how special needs teachers can become effective agents of curriculum change and development. There is insufficient time and space within the confines of this chapter to allow a full exploration of the issues involved in managing change. However, I feel that a logical development of support work will bring the special needs teacher right out of the cupboard to take part in management decisions with the school. Lieberman (1986) notes -

> "In many cases we find that change efforts have been successful due to some type of collaborative relations between participating parties." (p.5)

Golby and Gulliver (1979) suggest that to be effective the remedial teacher should be an agent of curricular and institutional change, modifying both the media and content of teaching. To enable this to happen it is important that some of the issues involved are explored. Ainscow (1984) reviews some of the difficulties of working as a change agent in special education settings and Hopkins (1986) provides a comprehensive summary of the literature on leadership and process of change. He points out that

> "There is ample evidence to suggest that top-down approaches to change are not as effective as once was thought." (p.83)

The special needs teacher is in the ideal position to sensitise colleagues and together they can work on developing the whole school's response to special educational needs. Argyris (1970), Lippitt (1978), Hoyle (1976) and Bolam (1975) all have valuable contributions to make in guiding such development. Bolam suggests a framework which highlights the interactive nature of the change process and Fullan (1982) suggests that change can take from three to five years to effect, a point worth remembering for those of us who are impatient for development.

Conclusion

For too long special needs teachers have seen their role as one which is limited to dealing with individuals or small groups of children. It is my belief that whilst much valuable work was done at this level, it rarely informed the practice of subject specialist colleagues. Indeed the presence of the traditional remedial department may even have been a discouraging factor in the development of flexible whole school responses.

Current initiatives, particularly those involving cooperative work between special needs teachers and their colleagues, together with developments such as Technical, Vocational Education Initiative (T.V.E.I.), Low Achievers Project (L.A.P.), General Certificate of Secondary Education (G.C.S.E.), Certificate of Pre-Vocational Education (C.P.V.E.) and their associated new approaches to assessment provide special needs teachers with the valuable opportunity of getting involved in the curriculum development debate within their schools.

I am not suggesting that all special needs teachers have the necessary skills, expertise or inclination to work in a consultative capacity and it would be naive to assume that such a way of working is the only way forward. Consideration will still need to be given to developing the existing skills of special needs teachers as well as looking at approaches which will enable them to become more effective at supporting colleagues and sharing perspectives with them. Although the INSET and initial training implications are considerable, they will have to be tackled, because the development of true partnership is unlikely to occur without adequate preparation.

In spite of the above cautionary words I still feel that the time is right for special needs teachers to come out of the cupboard and to parade their skills on a wider stage. Our main objective should become the development of flexible whole school approaches to special educational needs. This is more likely to be achieved if we are prepared to work as closely with our colleagues in the future as we have done with our pupils in the past.

Chapter Seven

STUDENTS WITH SPECIAL NEEDS IN FURTHER EDUCATION

Alastair Kent

1. Introduction

It is a relatively recent innovation for mainstream Colleges of Further Education to provide opportunities for students with special needs to attend either as students on traditional courses or on specially established courses for specific groups. As recently as 1976, Green and McGinty, in an unpublished survey for the Warnock Committee, found that only a small proportion of colleges were making any systematic provision for students with special educational needs.

The situation today is much changed although still patchy. Preliminary results from a survey carried out by the National Bureau for Handicapped Students for the D.E.S. indicate that the majority of colleges are making some form of provision, and that there are many thousands of students with a wide range of special needs currently attending mainstream Colleges of Further Education. Despite this vast increase, the pattern of provision varies enormously between colleges, and it is often more a matter of luck than for any other reason that a particular individual may be able to attend his or her local college. Few, if any, offer anything like a comprehensive range of opportunities comparable with that available at the nationally known pioneers in this work such as North Nottinghamshire College of Further Education.

A number of factors have combined to generate the impetus necessary to bring about this development. Not least among these has been the general increase in levels of youth unemployment, which has had a disproportionately great effect on school leavers with special needs. Between 1980 and 1982 the growth in numbers of registered unemployed disabled young people was 58% - from 20,700 to 32,600 (N.A.C.E.D.P. 1985). Currently school leaver unemployment affects about 5 in every 10. For those with special needs the figure is more like 8 in 10. In the early seventies, little if any consideration was given to extending education beyond statutory school-leaving age for school leavers with special needs, except as a last resort for the more severely disabled for whom a place in a residential college might be sought. The sharp decrease in employment opportunities puts schools and specialist careers officers under increasing pressure to "do something", and often they have turned to local F.E. colleges to meet this need. The more entrepreneurial college principals were quick to see the opportunity provided by the availability of Manpower Services Commission money through the (then) Youth Opportunity Programme to establish short (13-week) Work Introduction Courses as a response to this demand, thereby giving students with special needs, usually those with moderate learning difficulties or mild behaviour problems, a toe hold in the F.E. colleges. In addition, parental and student aspirations were rising, and the lead taken by some of the more committed colleges provided a spur to those still unsure of the relevance of the college environment to students with special needs.

Once students with special needs had established their presence in college, it quickly became apparent that the limitations imposed by the conditions attached to M.S.C. funding precluded an adequate response by the college, and there was a move to develop longer (L.E.A. funded) courses.

2. School and College - Contrasting Approaches to Teaching and Learning

In any mainstream college of further education, the majority of students with special needs will have moderate learning difficulties and will probably have received much of their schooling in special schools or units. Although special schools vary, the majority of them share many assumptions about the curriculum characterised by Hegarty et al (1981) as "basic skills plus general enrichment". This is based on a deficit model of special needs, is restricted in breadth and places a heavy emphasis on teacher-pupil interaction, with subject matter playing a subsidiary role. This model is in stark contrast to traditional practices in further education, which had stressed the teacher's mastery of his/her subject matter, giving high priority to the imparting of skills and knowledge to the student, but paying little heed to the quality of the interaction between teacher and the taught. Green amd McGinty (1979) highlight the need to integrate these two approaches. It is not enough for the teacher to have a grasp of the subject, or to understand the learning needs of the students. If progress is to be made then both these factors must be interrelated. For some lecturers, particularly those with experience in traditional F.E., this may represent a considerable threat, and the manager charged with responsibility for development of special needs work must be aware of this and provide support and opportunities for staff development to enable those new to this way of working to develop the necessary skills and confidence.

Traditionally, further education colleges have tended to operate as self-replicating systems, in that cooks turned out cooks, engineers engineers, secretaries secretaries and so on. Students with special needs in college did not fit this model, and in the early stages of this work the response of many colleges was to import teaching staff from special schools (and often the Ladybird book and plastic money as well) to provide what was in effect a continuation of special schooling. This was (and too often still is) usually in separate premises - a mobile classroom or an annexe - and made little or no impact on the general running of the college. The staff thus imported often had very little understanding of the way in which further education colleges operate. Such notions as, for example, "contact hours" or "servicing" were foreign to them. Equally they brought with them ideas unfamiliar to many in F.E., such as parental involvement or negotiation about curricular aims, and expected the involvement of outside agencies like the Careers Service or Social Services as essential members of the planning team for working out responses to individual students' needs.

Too often the ex-special school teacher has arrived in a college of further education with a brief "to start up special needs work", and been faced with the in-at-the-deep-end model of course development. In such a situation the possibility of effective working is almost completely eliminated, and the first priority for the naive course tutor has to be a damage limitation exercise which ensures survival and hopefully does not alienate too many colleagues on whom the special needs staff will depend for servicing and support. If this is to be avoided, the Head of Department or other manager must take steps to prepare the ground before the new members of staff commence, and to support them once in post.

There are a number of key elements in this process. Colleges ought not to decide to accept students with special educational needs unless they have followed a careful process of planning and consultation within and without college. External agencies who should be included in this operation include, for example, on the supply side, relevant teachers, careers officers and educational psychologists, and on the output side, Y.T.S. scheme managers, careers officers (again) and social services staff. In this way it ought to be possible for college senior management to produce a clear picture of the type of special need they might be asked to meet, the resource implications, and where a college course might fit into the overall pattern of provision in an area.

Armed with this information, the Head of Department or other manager is in a position to liaise and negotiate with colleagues before the more junior members of staff are in post, and to establish a modus operandi which leaves them to fill in the details. For this to happen in practice, careful attention must be paid to developing systems for gathering information and communicating it to those who need to know. Without this it is possible, as happened recently in one F.E. college, for a business studies lecturer to arrive for the first session of a B.T.E.C. course and be faced by four blind students, complete with Perkins Brailers, sitting in her group and expecting to be taught; or for a special needs lecturer to attempt to gain access to computing facilities for a group of students with moderate learning difficulties and be refused outright by the section head on the grounds that he didn't want "those loonies messing up my equipment".

Equally important is the development of a proper orientation and induction programme for staff new to F.E. and new to the particular college. Such a programme, although free-standing and self-contained, should not be the sole manifestation of senior management support for new staff, but a part of a continuing programme of support for professional and personal development. It must tackle staff attitudes and expectations as well as impart skills and knowledge if the reaction outlined above is to be prevented.

A further complication to the smooth and progressive development of special needs work in further education has been the use made by some colleges of this work as a way of preserving the jobs of lecturers faced with slack time-tables as a result of the decline in traditional areas of work-apprentice training and other day release courses - brought on by the sharp rise in unemployment over the last decade. Although often highly capable in their own field, such individuals frequently approached students with special needs with a feeling of ignorance and apprehension that was not calculated to permit the development of the students' full potential or capitalize on the opportunities presented by the college environment.

Paradoxically, once the barriers erected by staff redeployed to special needs work have been broken down, they often make excellent contributions to students' programmes. Such individuals have been used to taking an "industrial" approach to teaching, and thus transfer very appropriately to special needs courses, in that such an approach is task-orientated and has very specific aims and definable, comprehensible results. Teaching is also often in a practical environment and the desired outcomes can be clearly understood by both teacher and student alike, e.g. "At the end of the sessions the student will be able to use a tenon saw to cut a piece of timber on a pre-existing line." Also the more overt link between in-college activities and the world of work can give such staff an enhanced credibility and improve student motivation.

If the college manager is to capitalise on these talents then a way of giving such staff the skills, attitudes and expectations that will enable them to manage confidently and competently in their new role will have to be devised. In-service courses, for example the City and Guilds 731/4 "Teaching Students with Special Needs in Further Education", have a role to play, as does the F.E.U./N.F.E.R. (1985) teaching pack "From Coping to Confidence". One of the most effective ways of overcoming resistance and/or anxiety is by peer support and a team approach. Often special needs courses are double staffed, permitting a 1:6 staff/student ratio in practical sessions. In this context the redeployed craft lecturer and the special needs lecturer can work in parallel, the one initially concentrating on skill training, the other responding to the demands made by the student's special needs. As they each gain in confidence about the other's area, so the lines of demarcation will blur. Consideration should also be given to the use of space. For example, colleges often have open-plan workshops or practical areas, within which several groups may be operating simul-taneously but each on different courses. Planning a special needs group in such an environment will do a lot to allay suspicion and alter attitudes. This can only happen, though, if those with management responsibility want it to and are prepared to make the necessary arrangements to allow this incidental learning to occur.

When faced with the problem of what to do to fill a slack timetable, the head of department ought to resist the temptation to use compulsion when allocating lecturers to special needs work. It has to be OK to say "No". Knowing that this option exists, few people actually take it in practice: somehow staff are able to see that a basis for development exists and that, despite first impressions, their previous experience is relevant and provides a foundation to be built upon.

Barriers to Progress

The situation facing many colleges accepting students with special needs is one pregnant with possibilities, but also fraught with pitfalls. To exploit the former but avoid the latter calls for considerable skill in the management of people, policies and procedures. On the positive side, a place at college offers students with special needs the opportunity to learn in a wide range of settings - industrial, commercial and technical. If this is to happen then many barriers must be either overcome or circumvented, including resource and staff limitations, the lack of teacher education in F.E. and most important of all the attitudinal barriers which would prejudge and prohibit students from making their full contribution to college life and developing their abilities to the full. To overcome this, progress must be made on a number of fronts simultaneously, viz:-

    a. The Curriculum
    b. Staffing and staff development
    c. Co-ordination and communication

        i) within the college and
       ii) without the college.

The difficulties are further compounded by the low status given to special needs work by the Burnham system of grading courses. This results in a severe restriction in the number of posts above LI or LII level, and can place responsibilities upon the shoulders of staff at relatively low levels in the college hierarchy which would not normally be assumed until more senior positions, with resultant increase in stress and diminution of bargaining power when negotiating, for example, for access to resources, improvements in staffing levels or for higher priority to be given to special needs work as opposed to other areas of college activity. The basic aim of work with all students in further education is to promote personal and intellectual development, and to prepare to a greater or lesser extent for adult life. For students with special needs this goal includes -

    preparation for employment
    preparation for daily living
    preparation for use of free time
    preparation for further education or training.

If the F.E. curriculum for students with special needs is to allow the possibility of integration and to permit progression where appropriate to mainstream courses, then curriculum development must be carried out in the context of a common core of aims and objectives. This principle is acknowledged by the F.E.U. (1981) and the M.S.C., and has been developed into a curriculum framework for the Certificate of Pre-Vocational Education (C.P.V.E.) (Joint Board 1984) which arose from a general consensus about the kind of 16+ education that ought to be available to all young people.
This kind of development is a potentially threatening one for many college lecturers, more used to working with received curricula than to planning, adapting and developing individually based and negotiated schemes of work. The challenge for senior management is to provide such individuals with the skills and competencies to cope with confidence with this new and relatively unfamiliar way of

working.

A survey published by the National Bureau for Handicapped Students (1986) revealed the 80% of Lecturers Grade I or II undertake the following duties in addition to teaching:

Developing courses
Interviewing students and assessing
  their suitability for courses
Liaison with feeder schools
Liaison with parents
Liaison with outside agencies - social workers,
  careers officers, education psychologists
Organising work experience
Arranging industrial and educational visits
Timetabling
Ordering equipment and materials
Arranging transport for students
Counselling for students
Writing reports on students

In addition, 50% of LI/LII lecturers undertook the following:

Organising parents' evenings
Acting as specialist adviser for
  special needs students in college
Answering written requests for
  information from other colleges
Taking part in regional or national
  developments on provision
Health and Safety
Liaison with M.S.C. local staff

Many of these are not normally undertaken by lecturers on this grade.

A Strategy for Change

Colleges of Further Education are complex institutions and any lecturer faced with a range of duties in addition to his or her normal class contact hours, which tend to infinity, may feel tempted to become the "hero-innovator" and attempt to tackle both the organisational constraints and the practical problems which will inevitably arise to impede progress towards the desired goal. The normal response of the college to such a non-specific dispersed assault is, as Georglades and Phillimore (1975) predict, to eat hero innovators for breakfast and continue on its previously determined path without even a perceptible increase in flatulence to mark our hero's passing.

Thomas and Jackson (1986) suggest a framework for the

management of change which may lessen the difficulties associated with the introduction of special needs work in a mainstream setting. Their model, although specifically developed with the needs of schools in mind, is equally applicable to the F.E. college. The major features are summarised thus:

1. Present crucial aspects of information in a concise and digestible form.

2. Identify everyone likely to be affected by change and canvass their opinion. People are more likely to support if they feel that they have been consulted and involved.

3. Modify the scheme to take account of the outcomes of this consultation.

4. Make the scheme flexible and adaptive.

5. Provide support for individual members of staff through interest groups or by other means to permit the sharing of ideas and the venting of frustration, and also to prevent feelings of isolation.

6. Start with the committed rather than with the dyed in the wool reactionary whose notion of special educational needs begins with those who won't get their A-levels.

7. Change attitudes by personal approaches to colleagues rather than by assertively marketed "whole college" publicity packages which are likely to be of little impact and quickly forgotten.

Central Support: Local Initiatives

The identification by the Further Education Unit (F.E.U.) of special needs work as one of the areas for particular attention, and the appointment of development officers with responsibility for overseeing curriculum development projects in this area has been a major factor in legitimising this work in F.E. Although concentrating initially on students with moderate learning difficulties (see for example "Skills for Living", F.E.U., 1982) more recent projects (F.E.U., 1986; F.E.U. in progress) have highlighted the ways in which colleges can respond to students with other forms of special educational needs, and the staffing and resource implications of this response.

The development programmes for students with special needs in college have an influence on many areas of activity both within and without college. For maximum effectiveness, colleges ought to articulate a policy framework within which this development can occur, rather than permitting it to grow in an ad hoc manner. Such a policy will permit staff with responsibility for managing this growth to:

a) prepare colleagues, parents, students and others for the inherent possibility of this work;

b) prepare the college systems for the impact of new ideas and practices;

c) reduce the negative aspects of the college's systems and the staff and students - for example, the demands of college administration systems on students with poor literacy or communication skills, or the timetabling of specialist teaching facilities to permit or prohibit access by students with special needs.

The importance of a policy framework has been recently highlighted by N.A.T.F.H.E. (1985), who state that:

"the central aim of such policies should be to maximise the possibilities of individuals of integration with fellow-students in the context of 'mainstream' provision: special courses will often be necessary, but as a means to an end rather than as an end in themselves. It follows that physical integration into college premises rather than separate annexes should be the aim of all L.E.A. policies" (para. 6).

This apparently simple, would-be commonsense statement poses a major challenge to all those involved in the planning, resourcing and delivery of services to students with special educational needs in further education. The question is: can they rise to meet it?

College Structures: The Shock of the New

Other, novel influences also affect the pattern of provision and the work of the providers in F.E. These include the involvement of parents and the close liaison necessary with other professionals - often unfamiliar figures for the "traditional" F.E. lecturer whose job was to teach skills not people. Such professionals may include the specialist careers officer, the educational psychologist, the social worker and the school doctor.

Firstly, let us consider parents and their involvement in the education of their children post-16. The Warnock Report (D.E.S., 1978) stressed the importance of parents as partners in the education process (para. 9.1), but despite this and other official nods in the direction of parental involvement (D.E.S., 1977, 1978) the evidence (Smith, 1980) suggests that many teachers are still reluctant to take parental involvement seriously. Although Marra (1984) proposes one model for involving parents on a partnership basis in the education of their children, Hartley (1986) identifies some of the very real consequences for professionals in terms of their own "professionalism" and "expertise" should these be adopted without reservation. Nowhere is this more apparent than in F.E., where parents are not usually included in discussion of their child's future, for students are expected to be responsible for themselves. Hutchinson (1985) questions how far we may be perpetuating the notion of 'special needs' by setting up parents' evenings, workshops and so on; yet without the active support and co-operation of parents, the curricular aims outlined above are likely to be frustrated, and the successful transition to adulthood that is the goal of so many students with special educational needs in F.E. will be thwarted.

With regard to the involvement of "other professionals", colleges of F.E. often lack the necessary formal structures to ensure co-ordination and co-operation. Historically the development of provision for students with special needs in F.E. has been characterised by the presence of key individuals as the "hero-innovators" referred to above - whose enthusiasm and commitment has allowed nothing to deter them. If we are to move on from this position, and common justice demands that we do, then the FE system must accept the legitimacy of the demands made by students with special needs and see them as a normal part of the student body, and make the appropriate institutional response. If a pupil statemented under the 1981 Act continues in school to the age of 19, the procedures specified by the Act continue in effect. However, if the meeting of that pupil's special educational needs involves a transfer to F.E., then the statement lapses, and services hard-pressed to meet their statutory responsibility will often withdraw. With remarkable prescience the Warnock Committee recommended (10-42) that every college should appoint a co-ordinator for students with special needs with sufficient status and an appropriate position within the college hierarchy to ensure that he/she can influence college policy and provision and ensure liaison with other agencies. Within college the co-ordinator needs to be seen to influence the decision-making process, for example by sitting on the academic board and other major college committees, and without college her/his expertise must be such as to demand an input, for example the statutory re-assessment at 13+ required by the 1981 Act.

Recently policy developments, for example the Technical & Vocational Education Initiative (T.V.E.I.) and the Certificate in Pre-Vocational Education (CPVE) have stressed their applicability to students of all abilities. This may have been merely loose wording on the part of the speech writers at the D.E.S. or M.S.C., but nevertheless it provides an ideal opportunity for those concerned with the education of students with special needs in F.E. to ensure the attainment of two key goals long held in special schools as axiomatic but relatively new in F.E.; these are negotiated curricula and individual learning. At the same time the opportunity is there to end the isolation of many courses specifically developed for students with special needs by incorporating the opportunity for progression onto mainstream courses by students successfully completing such prevocational pro- grammes, thereby ensuring real, functional integration instead of stopping at locational or social integration alone.

T.V.E.I., with its concept of a four-year curriculum spanning the ages 14 - 18, provides an ideal opportunity to bridge the school/college divide, whilst at the same time circumventing the legislative ineptitude which allows the statement and its consequent resources and services to lapse upon transfer from school to college. It also highlights the key role of the college co-ordinator if this is to work effectively. This idea has been expanded in the recent publication by the F.E.U./S.C.D.C. (1985) of the document "Supporting T.V.E.I."

In its early stages, F.E. frequently copied the special schools in its attempt to respond to students with special educational needs - even down to importing the Ladybird books and plastic money and poaching the leavers' group tutor from the local school for pupils with moderate learning difficult- ies. The C.P.V.E. and T.V.E.I. have altered this and permitted F.E. teaching to come of age, and to emphasize that it has a significantly different role to play in the educa- tion of these students. Now that permission has been given it remains to be seen whether college management can grasp the opportunity thus presented and enable the necessary structures to emerge that will translate rhetoric to reality.

Finally, the role of the voluntary sector as an agent of change should not be either overlooked or underestimated. For many years the residential specialist colleges have been the only avenue to post-school education for many students with special needs. Consistently the colleges have asserted the potential of students with severe and profound disabilities to benefit from further education, and provided a model for the maintained sector to emulate. For a minority of students, the voluntary colleges still provide the best possible form of provision (see Kent, 1986). Recent developments such as the F.E.U./Nottinghamshire County Council project on "Transition to Adulthood" at North Nottinghamshire College of Further Education has shown that, given the resources and the will, it is possible for the maintained sector to go some way at least towards accommodating even those with severe

121

physical disabilities and additional handicaps. Nevertheless, it is an all too common experience for young people
with severe disabilitites to find that they are limited by
the perceptions of others - be they local college or
community - once they leave the supposedly segregated and
restricting environment of their specialist college.

In the space of a brief chapter it is possible only to
outline some of the issues which will have to be faced by
college management charged with responsibility for development of provision for students with special educational
needs, and to suggest possible methods for the resolution of
potential problems and pitfalls. In this context it is
helpful to consider the college as a bar of iron, within
which the various atoms are all pointing in different directions at random. It is the responsibility of management to
act as a magnet aligning the atoms and ensuring that the
resultant force is channelled in the direction of implementing the policy of the college. It should also ensure the
right of access for students with special educational needs
to college based F.E. provision.

Chapter Eight

WHAT'S THE JOB ABOUT?

Sue Knight, Rosalie White, Barbara Tyler
and Brian Steedman

Four special needs teachers have contributed to this
chapter. Each of them has had specialist training in the
education of children with special needs and now has a
support and advisory role; some of them have direct teaching
responsibilities, too. Their work settings are, however,
different from one another. Here they describe their
responsibilities in terms of a "typical" day; there is of
course no such thing, but these four accounts by practising
professionals provide a picture of what is entailed in doing
their particular jobs.

Sue Knight, Special Educational Needs Support Service,
Bedfordshire.

To some people, a drive of twenty miles each way to work
would be a chore, but it is the only time in the day when I
can think almost undisturbed. Today, the half an hour or
so drive is extremely important. At nine-thirty I have
organised a team leaders' meeting and need to be particularly
well prepared. I am the Co-ordinator of the Special
Education Support Service. There are five teams covering the
whole of Bedfordshire with a total of twenty-five teachers
plus myself. Today I am meeting with the five team leaders.
There are three major items on the agenda: the Support
Service Evaluation Questionnaire, Middle School provision and
next year's inservice education programme.
The most sensitive issue today revolves around this
first item, the Support Service Evaluation Questionnaire. The
Education Committee had requested that all teachers be
canvassed for their views about the effectiveness of the
Service, in order that they may presumably judge whether or
not we are 'value for money'. There is always rivalry
between groups set up in this manner, but this document has
heightened the tensions. I must be unbiased, cool, tough,
but entertaining today. I remember once hearing a psycholo-

gist talking about gifted children and appealing to the audience not to mistake popularity with leadership qualities. I wonder sometimes whether my leadership rests too heavily on being popular - but I will perform today.

I arrive on time but have to ignore the telephone messages on my desk. It is also necessary to ask the receptionist not to disturb us with messages or everyone will be edgy.

A prompt start, and the evaluation is the first item on the agenda. There is much discussion about how head teachers have misunderstood the questions and a funny story from Marjorie about the head teacher whose comment was "The first time that I met anyone from the Support Service was when they came to bring this questionnaire". Evidently, Marjorie and some of her team have been working in the school for some time but the head teacher knows them as "the Remedial Team".

This breaks the ice and slowly other team leaders retell similar stories. Eventually we begin to see some clear ways to present the information culled from the questionnaire. As we look more closely at the replies we can see a strong pattern of support for our work from the schools and tensions begin to dissipate. So far so good.

The next item - Middle School Provision - is always a thorny problem, but one that we feel committed to do something about. Very useful discussion ensues. I am aware that with five very vociferous and capable people, it is necessary to be strict about chairing the discussion or tempers will rise if points are lost or each person isn't given a fair hearing. I must always try to make notes and most importantly give credit where it is due. I am beginning to feel tired but Marie can be relied on to announce coffee at a useful point. While we drink our coffee I must remember to ask about individuals within the teams. I try to visit each team every half term, and then once a term we have a full team 'Study Day', but even so it is very easy to lose track. Has Mandy had her baby yet? Is Jackie recovering from her hysterectomy? At least now that we have some men in the team, ailments are becoming more interesting.

Back to business, and the final item on the agenda is the Inservice Programme for next year. During this item we get a little show of temperament. The Inservice Programme carries high status and by implication so do the people who contribute to it. If the skills of one member of the team are more in demand than the others', then this can cause unnecessary competition. We must bear in mind the needs of schools, and guard against providing training that we prefer, without necessarily meeting the needs of the customers. The debate gets heated, but then it's out of disagreement that we get creative growth. I must tie the problem up quickly and move on, but be on the look-out for any casualities caused by this little skirmish.

Lunch is usually good and it is at this time that we repair any damaged egos from the meeting. We usually get a quick pub lunch and alcohol takes over where management leaves off. The Authority is lucky to have such a committed group and I feel good when I get the strength of the team around me. Leadership at a distance is hard, but the rewards are great at meetings like these. I must be sincere but I am worried about how many times I hear myself saying "That sounds exciting". I would make a wonderful stand-in for Hughie Green.

Time to go. I have to give a talk to probationary teachers this afternoon. I am 'on' at 3.30 for twenty minutes, but must be there for two o'clock. By the time I get up to speak, these new teachers have sat through the Multi-ethnic Support Team, the Inspection and Advisory Service and the Careers Service. The audience are looking decidedly 'jaded'. A circus act is called for. I do a 'from the heart' performance - peppered with some working class restricted code; they like it. Finally questions are called for and, of course, because I was the last speaker, I field most of the these. Everybody is relieved when it is 4.15 and tea is ready.

I cannot stay for tea because I have an appointment at a local school for 4.30, where I am supporting the Special Needs Co-ordinator with her school-based initiative. On the recommendations of our Chief Education Officer, all schools are encouraged to develop the role of the Special Needs Co-ordinator. A major inservice training initiative was developed in conjunction with two local colleges. The course which qualifies for a Regional Certificate operates on a twenty full day release programme. At the end of the course each student is required to develop a school-based awareness programme of about six sessions. Each course must be individually developed with the strengths and weaknesses of each school taken into consideration. This particular school has a newly-appointed head and a very earnest Special Needs Co-ordinator. The rest of the staff must be unique in their lack of concern for special needs. They had been heard to say, in excuse for their reluctance to involve themselves in this area, that they were 'not trained to teach pupils with learning difficulties'. They won't make that mistake again; this keen head teacher has seized the opportunity to congratulate them on their honesty and rectified the situation with this school-based initiative. The head teacher is going to need all the support he can get. The staff are there in body but not in mind. I am tempted to muse over how industry would train people to deal with reluctant customers, but then we are not in the selling game - or are we?

I arrive home at above 6.30 and Tone, my husband, is sitting with his knife and fork at the ready. God bless

Birdseye. Gosh, wouldn't it be easier if it was the other way round? Little wife sitting at home waiting for busy businessman husband to arrive. The difference is that little wife would be waiting with a nice soothing Martini and husbands wait with anxious expressions. Ah well, I'll join the feminists when I get the time.

The Home Tutors' support group meeting at 7.45 saps the last bit of energy. How do you support a home tutor who has been working extremely well with a very difficult fifteen-year-old until the child confesses something about himself that the tutor cannot handle? The boy has become extremely abusive and is now deemed out of control again.

Tomorrow will be better.

*   *   *   *   *

Rosalie White, Special Needs Co-ordinator in a comprehensive school, London Borough of Havering.

I choose to begin today slowly and gently as every day, imagining time is my slave because the pace certainly hots up later. A leisurely breakfast and then I slide into the driving seat; on goes a tape of love songs. The rich throaty voice creates a sensation of being bathed in warm chocolate. Just the right mood. Oh God no! I promised to take a garden table and four chairs today for the school play.

After some strenuous efforts to unclip the back seats and force the piece of furniture into the unyielding vehicle, I drive off with one chair leg ominously close to my nose. Mood broken.

As I approach the comprehensive school where I work, the navy-blue uniforms grow thicker along the pavements and coagulate around the gates. As sole member of the Special Needs Department, I make a lot of friends among the pupils and four of the faithful scamper over to the car as it stops. 'Can we take anything in for you Miss?' Vatsal smiles as he jostles with Jason. 'Cor, look at that lot Jess'. Jess and Lynn's eyes sparkle - they can use the excuse of carting the furniture to bunk off assembly.

The props unloaded and in position on the stage of the drama room, I notice that someone has already written something rude on my table. Jeremy Briggs is a ... What? Oh well, they say it isn't harmful.

A phone call awaits me. It is Colin's dad confirming that there really is something wrong with his son. Over the years Colin has gained a reputation for losing a record number of exercise books, leaving his house empty with front and back doors wide open and neglecting a succession of toasters, electric fires and bath taps. But this time it really is serious. He left his A.T.C. boots out in the rain last night. As Colin lives and breathes for A.T.C., his dad and I know we have something big on our hands. I must see Colin as soon as possible. This is a job for Superteach. I wonder if the problem is what I think it is; surely not so soon. Lessons first though, then Colin.

My room is warm and bright, quite inviting, but I watch my three pupils walk nonchalantly to and fro past the door, not wanting to be seen entering. They wait until their peers are gone. At last they come in, hands in pockets. As we recall the story they were reading last week, they begin to perk up. It has reached an exciting stage and they are keen to read on. During the first sessions, digital watches would be consulted regularly but now time goes unheeded. Heads are bent earnesly over the large print. The gripping tale unfolds in faltering phrases.

Sound of the pupils next door on the move indicate the end of lesson. 'We'll just finish this page then,'I say. 'Oh Miss!'comes the despondent chorus. Darren jumps up and rushes towards the door clutching the book. I chase after him and head him off at the door grabbing the book. He says he wants to take it home and finish the story.

'Oh no you don't,'I cry triumphantly, 'I need that book for my other group.' Hang on, what am I saying? Darren is a reluctant reader. I am supposed to be pushing books onto him! 'Oh go on then.'

The other two wail in protest. 'That's not fair Miss. If he can, why can't we?' Two more reluctant readers bite the dust.

Jane the computer teacher and I share a tea bag. We can't wait for the communal brew-up. She always has to dash back to her room to nurse a piece of software and I'm on break duty. I must see Colin.

Today is sunny, so most rooms are empty of pupils, just a few stragglers draped on radiators and Karen searching for me around the corridors. She comes to cry on me. This is a regular occurrence. She always chooses to cry on my right arm and several of my jumpers now have one sleeve shorter than the other. I must remember to wear them back to front to give the other sleeve a chance.

The cause of the anguish varies but today it's because her father has been horrible to her. He shouted, her boyfriend has noticed her spots and she won't live through the English oral exam. I juggle my cup in my left hand and attempt to wrap the wet arm around her. A few consoling words and the tears disappear until tomorrow.

No time to see Colin as the Special Needs Adviser is here for her weekly session. We exchange news about the pupils I see, discuss different approaches to be tried and laugh about the questions asked in a meeting last week. In walks the Educational Psychologist. I wish they hadn't laid rubber flooring outside my room: we would have heard him coming. He was the one asking the stupid questions we were laughing about. Oh no, this always happens. The representatives of these two support agencies glare at each other. They are going to start arguing again.

The first thrust is from the Special Needs Adviser on the inadvisability of descending on schools unannounced and without an appointment. A strong parry from the other to the effect that this is the new 'open' approach to Ed. Psyching. Their voices become raised and touch on matters of role, on territory and accusations of 'treading on people's toes'. I retreat and close the door quietly. I'll bring some coffee, that usually helps.

As I pass the maths class next door, I reflect that I could have used this time to work with some of the weaker pupils in their lesson.

In the staffroom I wait for the kettle to boil. Mr. Davis admonishes a pupil at the open doorway. 'Don't be so childish, Brown,' he barks. 'But Sir, I am a child.' Mr. Davis's shoulders droop.

'Worried parent for you on line one,' the Secretary trills. 'It's Mrs. Parks.'

'Hello Miss. My Anthony's worried about all that sex you were doing there yesterday.'

'I'm sorry Mrs. Parks but I don't know what sex you mean.'

I begin to wonder whether I should spend more time in the staffroom at lunchtimes. Perhaps I am out of touch with what is going on these days.

'You and Mr. Gardner were doing it yesterday in Biology.' I hurriedly attempt to recall the events of yesterday. Of course . . .

'Oh yes, you mean the First Year lesson on Reproduction.' I know Anthony well. He has epilepsy and has difficulty with some concepts of space and time and quite a few more come to think of it.

'That's right Miss. You know he's got this big problem about time Miss, well I keep telling him, all that sex is not for now Anthony, it's for when you're a man. Only he's worried about what you want him to do for homework Miss.'

'Please tell Anthony not to worry, there isn't any homework this week.' Perhaps we'll have to rethink that lesson plan.

I meet Colin coming towards me along the corridor. I can tell by his strutting walk and by the shiny upswept hair that is usually an unruly mop. Even before I ask him, I know he's in love again.

Lunchtime and the regular meeting of the Duke of Edinburgh Award group. In an attempt to look the part I don training shoes and sit on a desk with one leg swinging. I tie granny knots in a piece of rope and untie them again. This appears to give potential awarders confidence in me.

Fortunately, they will never have to rely on me supporting them on a cliff face, just for filling in application forms. No outdoor antics for me thank goodness.

Peace at last. Pupils strategically seated for their maths exam. No one too close to anyone else and just enough room between desks for me to roam around wearing the right expression - serious but tinged with encouragement. Young minds settle to work and I select a spot by the open windows where my back can be warmed by the sun.

Pupils look up, small eyes widen. 'Miss, Miss!' urgently.

'No talking' I snap.

'But MISS!' Fingers point. Behind me the light has faded. A swarm of bees rises outside the window. We all scramble to pull down the windows. We must have been quick; only a few bees are inside buzzing around the floor amidst the scattered exam papers. Ten minutes later a message comes from the office. Please close all windows, there's a swarm of bees in the tree outside.

For a fortnight I have phoned to plead with unwilling and unenthusiastic parents to come to a Parental Involvement in Reading meeting this evening. It is an experiment and tonight is very important to me; it must succeed. Anxiously I count the arrivals as they enter the specially smartened classroom. To make the atmosphere welcoming, tables have been pushed together and draped with a collection of table cloths. Tracey, one of the more flamboyant third year pupils, suggests we should have bowls of flowers. Too late I notice her purple head bobbing about in the rose border outside the Headmaster's office. Not a single rose is left unpicked. Books are spread about in casual profusion. The room resembles a tawdry restaurant with too many thick menus.

The silent mums and dads who submitted reluctantly to coming to the meeting are on first name terms. Arms are flung around each other, they screech with laughter as they read parts in a set of my plays (Reading age 7 to 9). It is nine thirty and they show no sign of leaving. I make two hasty reminders on my notes. **Don't** serve home made wine at the next meeting. **Do** say what time the meeting will end.

I arrive home yearning for fresh air. I will sit in the garden. I forget that my garden chairs are gone.

*   *   *   *   *

Barbara Tyler, Area Special Needs Support Teacher, Suffolk

The alarm goes off at 7.15 a.m. I wait for the clock in the hall to strike 7.30 before getting out of bed. From then on it's all systems go to get out of the house by 8.30! Today is Tuesday and I have have half an hour's journey to my first school. During breakfast I collect my thoughts, hastily make

a sandwich, ensure I have all the bits and pieces with me for
the day - including my shopping list for Sainsburys. I hope
to get there at the end of the day!

By 8.30 I am ready. My dear husband has got the Fiat
out of the garage. I say goodbye to the family and I'm away.
Driving along I concentrate on my first apppointment. This
morning I am due to see an eleven year old girl whose parents
think she might be dyslexic. This is a concern common to
many parents due, I believe, to publicity since the 1981 Act.
The drive to school is a comfortable one, no unforeseen
hazards, no long delays at traffic lights. I am on time - a
good start.

Anne-Marie is a delightful girl. She is well aware of
her difficulties with reading, writing and spelling. I give
her two tests that tell me something about her intellectual
ability (results are slightly below the mean). Reading and
spelling tests show that Anne-Marie has scores approximately
two years below her chronological age. I decide to give
Anne-Marie tests for short-term memory, sequencing and
perceptual skills. She scores reasonably well on all three.
I describe Anne-Marie to her head teacher as a girl with a
weakness in spelling and reading, but I would not label her
as being dyslexic. We discuss a programme of work. I leave
the school having agreed to meet her parents if the Head
feels it necessary.

My next appointment is at an upper school only five
minutes' drive away. I am due once again to see a probationary teacher at 10.30. This lass is very conscientious; she
usually has a long list of queries for me. I wonder what
will be on the agenda today. Liz is waiting for me. Straight
down to her needs, no time for chit-chat. We work our way
through her list: first a query about aims and objectives.
What are the differences, I ask myself? We look at her
records for the term; they are good. I am able to make a
few positive suggestions to improve the format. If only all
teachers kept detailed lessons notes like these! I
congratulate Liz. She needs this encouragement - morale is
rather low. Her life out of school hasn't been much fun.
Liz has had to start anew and it hasn't been easy. Money is
limited, but at least she has a few sticks of furniture now.
She is beginning to make friends too. Next on the list, a
query about the 'tearaways' in 4c. Oh that class! At least
the bête noire has been absent for two weeks. I feel the
relief in Liz's voice as she tells me this. We talk through
ways of coping with dear Sean. I suggest making contracts
with the lad. I hope this works.

Liz has a lesson at 11.30 and needs to put work on the
board. I go off to find Bob, the school's Special Needs Co-
ordinator. We have a brief chat about Liz; we both admire
her enthusiasm and willingness to learn. Bob and I have a
brief chat about Instrumental Enrichment. I tell him what is

130

going on in another school that has just started to use the materials. He asks me to arrange for him to visit.

Today I am having a working lunch in a primary school. A seven-year-old girl is causing concern. Claire is a well-developed child; she looks healthy but has co-ordination problems. She has been described to me as being very clumsy in class. Her work is messy and untidy. Writing and drawings are poor for a child of seven. She finds learning to read difficult. When I arrive at school, Claire is already out to play prior to lunch. The Head Teacher, class teacher and I observe her from the classroom window. She certainly walks with an 'odd' gait but this might be due to the boots she is wearing. Nobody wants to play with Claire. She resorts to thumb-sucking. Next she sits on a form with her feet tucked under her. I now understand what her class teacher means when she says she is a contortionist. I look again at samples of her work. What am I going to recommend? I believe we need a physiotherapist's assessment: Claire appears to have a poor body image and spatial problems. I agree with the Head Teacher to make the necessary arrangements.

As Claire's mother lives nearby, the Head is keen that I should see mother at once and explain my thoughts. I look at my watch; my stomach is rumbling and I'm very thirsty. In a weak moment I agree to the suggestion and bolt my salad sandwiches before Claire's mother arrives. She appears very promptly. We discuss Claire and her difficulties. Obviously Claire's lack of progress has been rather a shock to her parents. She is an only child and until she went to school, her parents weren't aware that her clumsiness wasn't anything but "normal". We agree that Claire is a puzzle. Mother welcomes anything to get to the root of the problem.

Already I am late for my afternoon appointment, but I console myself with the thought that my time has been well spent. Quickly I drive to my next school (another primary school) full of apologies and hoping that somebody will offer me a cup of coffee. The Head Teacher has been engrossed with two naughty five-year-olds and hasn't realised I was late. We close her office door and straight away begin to discuss the five boys she wants to consider for placement in our new area special class. All boys certainly appear to have multiple problems. I make a quick decision to look at the five in their classes. It isn't going to be possible to make detailed observations today but at least I will have met them. Before leaving the school at 3 o'clock I agree on a date at the beginning of next term when I can look at each child more closely.

I have an hour before a meeting some distance away. If I hurry, I can dash around Sainsburys. My luck is in. There is a space in the car park. I quickly get all I need, write a cheque and dump the goods in the boot, trying hard not to

scramble the eggs!
   I am expecting at least eight enthusiastic teachers at
my meeting - I am talking about children with special
educational needs and how they might be helped. This is the
first time I've talked to this group. I feel a little
apprehensive. I just hope the overhead projector is in place
after all the effort our secretary has put in to making the
acetate copies for my talk. Why did I worry? A warm welcome
awaits me; at last a cup of tea, plus cake, and the overhead
projector is in place! The group is lively, we have a good
discussion about support teaching: no resisters in this
group.
   It's 6.30 and my day in schools has ended. Home now to
unload the car and prepare supper. How glad I am to possess
a microwave. I should write two reports tonight but don't
feel like it. Perhaps tomorrow won't be so demanding;
certainly I have no appointments after school.
   At 9.15 I decide to wash my hair. Just as I am giving
my hair its second wash, my daughter calls me to take a
'phone call. So with dripping hair caught up in a towel, I
pick up the telephone. One of my support teachers needs some
immediate help. A frantic mother with a school-phobic child
wants to know where to go for help. I could tell her! But
no, I listen carefully, ask a few more questions and give her
the advice I feel she needs.
   Back in the bathroom I finish hair washing, hoping that
nobody else will need to make contact today. Tomorrow, not
many hours away, is another day.

*   *   *   *   *

Brian Steedman, Head of Department in a special school,
London Borough of Waltham Forest.

   Industrial action has made inroads into my working
arrangements, but normally I arrive at work at about 8.30. My
role breaks down into three categories. Firstly I am a
teacher, with a class of eight junior-age children with
behaviour problems each of whom spends up to five mornings
with me and the remainder of their school time in mainstream.
Secondly, I support the children and their teacher in mainstream schools. Thirdly, I supervise a department within my
school which consists of four and a half teachers and four
welfare assistants, working with thirty-two children.
Naturally enough the three parts of my job continually
overlap and confuse me. This is not aided by the absence of a
clear job description, especially in the school liaison part
of my work. There is therefore, no typical day.
   The day begins, quite often, with mild panic; someone
is absent and cover must be arranged, an urgent conference is
needed and just who will attend it must be decided. Letters

must be gone through and answered and time found to discuss with teachers urgent problems arising about children. I try as best I can to deal with these issues before 9.15 a.m. when the children arrive, but often they continue into the morning's teaching, and I juggle endlessly inside my head with a number of competing thoughts.

Quite often I will have a visitor in class: a mainstream teacher, a student or parent who will sit watching proceedings. I aim to preserve a calm and good-humoured classroom atmosphere. I greet all the children as they arrive at the department's entrance, by which time they will have already received at least three greetings. I see quickly who's got out of bed on the wrong side. Children tell me their preoccupations and we chat briefly, but quickly they settle to 'work'. I have no time to prepare in school. Everything is very quick and industrious, with occasional interruptions for further greetings. The task in hand continues until ten, by which time we have breakfast, prepared by Joan, my welfare assistant. Breakfast - simply tea and toast - continues until play at 10.26 a.m., and offers time to talk through problems and pleasures in as unforced a way as possible. Joan or I will prompt occasionally, but the emphasis is upon a free and nurturing experience which the children generally initiate. It contrasts sharply with academic time within which I am clearly directing and setting, pleasantly, the level of expectation. There are few problems in either setting: clearly defined practice and expectations combine with good humour and industry to create a cheerful, purposeful atmosphere. Where things break down, I use 'time out' in the short-term and reward for acceptable behaviour in the long-term to bring about change. The frightening and aggressive part of difficult children seems to me to be dealt with very easily, generally, while niggling, less disruptive problems remain over the long-term which rarely tax the functioning of such a small group. This, really, is the easy and most rewarding part of my day.

As Head of Department I supervise play in the morning, which enables me to have contact with all the children in a free and informal setting. Then, as play ends, I pass on to class teachers reports of indiscretions committed by children. Activities continue until noon when again classes eat as groups, with still the emphasis on free conversation. My class then travel by coach to their own schools.

Briefly I discuss the morning with Joan who goes to unwind in the 'Welfare Arms'. I remain 'on call' should the mid-day assistants require me, generally writing letters, reports, notes and being available for chats. Often I am interrupted by telephone calls from schools or parents for news, advice or complaint.

The afternoons are less clear-cut. I spend about two afternoons per week in mainstream schools - not enough -

though I am in contact more frequently by telephone and at conferences and reviews. Mondays and Thursdays feature department meetings after school and on Wednesdays I attend Senior Staff meetings. Other sub-committees involve me in development of the curriculum, in fund-raising and in organising the primary department's annual camp. I have a minimum of one school review or conference a week and, since many of our children are in the care of the Social Services Department, I attend child care reviews frequently. Especially in the winter months, such routines as might be apparent here are disrupted by the need to cover for absent colleagues. Additionally, I have to make observations of colleagues in class to offer advice, and this role has become much expanded in the absence of a staff tutor over the last year.

Contacts with schools are the most problematical part of my work. No formal arrangements exist, and over eight years I have worked out my own salvation. In some schools I have 'carte blanche' to go where I please; in others I am barely recognised. Besides helping a child I have therefore the aim of building bridges and enhancing my school's credibility. Unfortunately this can clash with my view of the child as only part of the problem. Primary teachers rarely share children, so are insulated somewhat from the perception that problem children are not necessarily problems for everyone. Frequently I find children burdened with inappropriate work and the calm and businesslike atmosphere at my own school is not always replicated. The split of the child's time between schools also creates organisational problems and makes difficulties for everyone in building relationships.

I try to avoid being cast as an expert, though often what I call the 'Ah!' factor makes people look up to me. There is a reluctance to see my role as being to transfer skills and perceptions rather than to solve problems. Schools have barely begun to take on board their responsibility for meeting special needs - how many mainstream schools have a copy of the Warnock Report, let alone a staff who have read it? Sometimes I find the role a lonely one for which I feel ill-prepared.

A sense of proportion generally reasserts itself and I plod on. I encourage teachers to look at their classroom organisation and style and to ensure that their curriculum is appropriate, especially for the child we share. I guide them to look at 'disruptive behaviour' dispassionately, and to define it behaviourally. I invite them to see their part in its occurrence, looking at what precedes it and proceeds from it. I offer to guide them in setting up reinforcement programmes, though I find insufficient teachers who make these methods their own and subsequently use them independently. I am sure there are better ways forward.

I get home at a variety of times, but I switch off very

easily. I rarely discuss school away from it but if someone
sets me off, then I'm very hard to stop.

Chapter Nine

INVESTING IN SUCCESSFUL PARENTAL PARTNERSHIP

Allan Sigston

Currently parental involvement is a high profile issue within Education from a number of perspectives. The extension of parental rights through legislation both within the mainstream and special sphere has arisen from philosophical arguments.

Another strand has been the growing body of educational practitioners who have noted the practical value of utilising parents' skills and energy to improve the efficiency of education. A place at which these two strands meet is in the management of schools; for it is in the devising of school policy that philosophy must face practicality.

In the long term greater parental involvement implies a shifting in roles and responsibilities between teachers and parents. Clearly parental involvement projects raise key management issues in relation to the introduction of institutional change and person management. The aim of this chapter is to describe a framework for planning and evaluating projects, whilst placing them within the wider contexts of educational reform and the development of school policy.

Parental Involvement over the last two decades

The Plowden Report (D.E.S. 1967) raised the notion of parents and teachers as equal partners. It stressed the importance of positive parental attitudes towards schooling and encouraged methods by which they could be fostered. At the lowest level it advocated a number of practical steps to furnish parents with basic information about their child's progress and the work of the school in general, through written reports, an annual (at least) parent-teacher consultation and other more open events. This period also saw a rapid growth of Parent-Teacher Association and School 'Friends' organisations, mainly for the purpose of fund raising.

In recent years the focus seems to have moved away from

schools fostering parental interest, toward encouraging educators to be more responsive to the wishes of parents. The 1980 Education Act gave parents the right to express a preference for a school at secondary transfer that Local Education Authorities had to pay heed to when allocating places. This Act also ensured that all schools' boards of governors had parent representation, following in part the recommendation of the Taylor Report (D.E.S.1977).

The 1981 Education Act drew substantially on the Warnock Report (D.E.S.1978) in according parents of children who may have Special Educational Needs rights related to the assessment process, including access to information, opportunities to contribute themselves and rights of appeal against decisions.

Almost universally, parents are concerned with their children's welfare and this seems reason enough to ensure they can take a full part in educational decision-making. They also have an intimate knowledge of their child at home, their likes and dislikes, worries, the times that s/he is most alert and so on. Anyone who has had cause to explore these sorts of issues with parents rapidly becomes aware of the richness and relevance of the information available. Their knowledge and commitment have been increasingly recognised as unharnessed strengths which can be mobilised through partnership with the professionals involved with the child.

In many respects the 'Special Needs' sector of education has led the way in this type of parent-teacher partnership. Perhaps one of the best examples is to be found in Portage Projects. Portage involves a home visitor calling on a family weekly, working out with parents what the child can and cannot do, jointly deciding on teaching priorities and planning precise teaching activities that will be carried out on a daily basis by the parent (Daly et al, 1985). In Portage, parents have the major say in deciding the child's curriculum, as well as taking on an explicit teaching role. Similarly, it is not uncommon for special schools to hold regular review meetings attended by parents, teachers and often other professionals at which curriculum goals will be decided upon through consultation with all these interested parties.

Within the mainstream of education the most obvious sign of this increased inclusion of parents in their children's education has been the resurgence of interest in 'home reading', following mainly from Tizard, Schofield and Hewison's (1982) work. While it cannot be said that parents are influencing curriculum content to the same degree as in the earlier examples, there is little doubt that the vast majority of parents perceive the mastery of reading as one of the principal goals to be achieved in the primary school years. Hence, there is already a concordance between teachers and parents on the importance of literacy within the curriculum.

137

Linking School Policy and Parental Involvement

The preceding review illustrates that parental involvement can take a variety of forms to meet different ends.
Wolfendale (1983) offers a classification of four general
areas for the inclusion of parents in schools that serves to
highlight the choices available to a school pursuing the
general goal of increased parental involvement. These areas
are:-

(i)   Concrete and Practical

This covers the ways in which parents may assist in
the supplementing of resources through fundraising and
voluntary help in classrooms, under the direction of
teachers.

(ii) Pedagogical and Problem solving

Typical activities in this area are 'parent evening'
discussions on children's strengths and matters of
concern and contributions to overcome them. It could
also cover co-tutoring where the parent takes on a
circumscribed teaching role as in the case of home
reading initiatives.

(iii) Policy and Governing

Here the focus is on parents contributing to decisions
affecting the school as a whole. At its most direct
this will be as a parent governor themselves, but in
order to exert a more representative influence there
is a need for wider consultative mechanisms.

(iv) Communal

If it is successfully to achieve partnership in this
respect, a school should address itself both to the
agreed needs of the children for whom it shares care
and the needs of parents themselves. This would
require schools to sample parental wishes and provide
learning opportunities to meet them.

While these areas serve the purpose of illustrating
different possibilities in the realm of parental involvement,
it is crucially important to recognise that initiatives in
any one of them will have ramifications for others. For
instance, a decision to fund-raise for cookery equipment or
reading schemes has a bearing on curriculum emphasis and
content; home reading schemes will raise consciousness about
the roles of parents and teachers, the provision of reading
materials and school reading policy. Even the presence of
classroom helpers provides the local community with an

informal source of information on the classroom environment.
The implications of this are that schools contemplating parent projects of all kinds need to consider the following points if they are to embrace fully the benefits of parental involvement. Firstly, the particular objectives to be achieved by the project and secondly, where these objectives fit within the longer term policy aims for developing the dialogue between home and school at all the levels described.

Management Consideration in Setting up a Parent Involvement Project

A first consideration when introducing an innovation into a school is that staff and resources will already be deployed to near their full capacity. The introduction of a new priority implies that something, somewhere, will need to 'give'. The full adoption of new practices therefore requires decisions about the redistribution of resources.

More fundamentally, Georgiades and Phillimore (1975) in a seminal paper entitled "The Myth of the Hero Innovator", stress the difficulties in bringing about significant changes in the practice of individuals within organisations. They note that in commercial and industrial organisations it takes three to five years for substantial changes to take place. Estimates of this order seem realistic or even optimistic with regard to schools. For example, primary schools that have taken on the Individualised Reading approach have typically found that it takes this sort of period from inception to when all staff are using it consistently. Likewise, secondary schools which have changed the way they assist children with literacy difficulties from withdrawal groups to support teaching in ordinary classes, generally take a number of years for such changes to become fully operational and widely accepted by staff.

The examples cited here stress the long term nature of change. The reality, of course, is that most attempts at innovation do not stay the course!

Management Strategies

The picture for introducing initiatives may appear bleak. Fortunately there seem to be a number of useful pointers on optimising the chances for success. A good starting point is the old maxim of "success breeds success". There is no advantage to be gained from a large scale project that flounders, whereas success on a small scale through a pilot project serves as a firm foundation for growth. Generally speaking this is most likely to arise from the work of a small and cohesive working group.

139

The points that follow may serve as a useful guide to the formation and maintenance of such groups.

1) Select a team which is likely to succeed. Indicators:

   - members who have initial interest or enthusiasm for the area;
   - members who are regarded as competent and effective by other staff;
   - members who have already shown good levels of co-operation;
   - members who have time available;
   - a sufficiently large number to share tasks.

2) Demonstrate the value/priority given to the project by:

   - ensuring an appropriate allocation of resources at outset;
   - protecting group members from other competing demands;
   - carrying out own actions promptly;
   - systematically disseminating information;
   - ensuring meetings are not postponed without good reason and plenty of notice.

3) Make meetings effective by:

   - facilitating the participation of all those attending: if necessary by supplementing questioning such as, "How do you feel about that?"
   - not making negative comments about suggestions raised (if necessary stress the advantage of alternatives);
   - trying to reach decisions by consensus;
   - keeping minutes with clear, agreed actions.

One danger of taking this line is placing the project solely under the ownership of the working group which is likely to lead to resistance to adopting its findings. Practical ways of countering this are through providing formal and informal invitations to comment on progress at various stages and making materials freely available. Another means entails emphasising the link between the project and the institution rather than the individuals working on it, for example by using the school name prominently on all products.

The Responsibility to Evaluate

It is apparent from earlier comments that innovation introduces new stresses into a system, bringing with it a responsibility on the manager to assess the project and satisfy all parties that resources are being used to good effect. Education is beset with different methodologies and philosophies and it is notable how little substantive data is available to support the arguments of opposing proponents.

The traditional stance of research involving matched control groups, under pure conditions remote from those actually found in schools, or of vast surveys producing probabilistic generalisations, has done little to influence classroom practice. However, along with many others, the author has found the Action Research model extremely helpful.

The main characteristic of Action Research is that it is a practical response to perceived needs within an institution. Instead of attempting to isolate the precise effects of individual variables, the researcher/practitioner is interested in both planning and evaluating interventions within the prevailing conditions.

Action Research is usually a co-operative venture arising from the shared recognition of a need, agreement about aims and accountable actions to achieve them. Thus it dovetails well with the type of working group advocated earlier, and for this reason the Action Research model has been elaborated to provide the framework that follows for designing and evaluating projects.

The exact steps in Action Research are broadly similar from author to author (e.g. Adelman, 1985). The terminology and steps used here seem well suited to school-based projects.

A Framework for Implementing and Evaluating Parent Involvement Projects

Step One - Needs Analysis

This involves compiling a comprehensive list of short-falls in current arrangements in the nominated area(s). Points may seem somewhat vague or ambiguous but this is not problematic at this stage. Often a single meeting will be sufficient.

Step two - Clarification and Data Collection

The areas of interest recorded on the agreed list are clarified so that data can be collected to get a definitive description of the current situation.

Step Three - Goal setting

The information collected in the previous step allows a more objective view of the school's needs. Through discussion it may seem realistic to focus on only some of these clarified needs. Once a decision has been made as to which will be acted upon, goals can be set which would indicate that the identified needs were satisfactorily met.

It is vital that these goals are stated in a way that

141

their attainment, or otherwise, can be verified.

Step Four - Intervention

Having established a baseline position and decided upon goals to work toward, the task at this stage is to instigate actions likely to lead to attainment of these goals. Ideas will be drawn from a wide variety of sources including academic research, other projects and common sense.

Whatever is decided upon must be feasible for other staff to take on at a later stage.

Step Five - Monitoring the Intervention

Clearly an intervention cannot be evaluated unless it has taken place. Once initiated, it is important to have some agreed means of knowing whether actions have been carried out. As well as helping people to 'keep to task', monitoring often reveals ways of carrying out tasks more efficiently.

Step Six - Evaluation

Evaluation is usually straightforward as it directly relates to the goals set in step three. Usually no special statistical analyses are required and where there are, relatively simple techniques are available. If goals have not been achieved it will be necessary to reconsider the appropriateness of the goals set, the intervention and its implementation (steps three, four and five).

Step Seven - From Project to Policy

Many schools have failed to negotiate this hurdle and as a result their efforts have only touched briefly a sample of pupils and parents instead of generating a repeated harvest. Successful policy development is evidenced by the widespread application of the methods and procedures within the school. If the goals have been achieved there is already a powerful argument for doing so.

There are a number of factors that can ease this transition. Staff are more likely to accept changes if they feel some shared ownership of the project thus far and if they are able to participate in decisions about how these will be implemented.

It is an often overlooked truth that people are more likely to act upon their own suggestions than on instructions from others. For the manager, this period of consultation involves shaping the offerings of the staff into practical actions.

The processes of monitoring and evaluation should continue although perhaps to a lesser degree than that in the

initial stages of the project.   The routine collection of
basic data will indicate whether the benefits of the project
are apparent for the larger body of pupils and parents.   It
also provides a prompt that helps to maintain changes in
staff and parent behaviour.   At this point the manager will
need to consider changes in current organisation and
responsibilities to free the necessary resources to maintain
adequately both the project and staff sensibilities!

Finally, it is important to take account of how the
changes adopted as a result of the project relate to other
aspects of home-school communication vis-a-vis the different
levels of parent involvement described earlier.   For example,
some schools have found that as a result of the introduction
of a home reading policy, parent consultation evenings have
become more focused on the curriculum than on personalities.
This has led in turn to requests for parental workshops on
different subject areas.

The Action Research model serves as a robust and
flexible planning framework.   It makes no extravagant claims
for providing universal truths, but indicates ways forward
that will bring about improvements within the school's
particular circumstances.   By implication the policy it
develops becomes part of a continuous process of reasoned
appraisal and informed change.

An Illustration of the Framework

To illustrate the approach, a project that the author
was associated with will be described (Sigston et al, 1984).
Over two years prior to the inception of the project the
junior school was developing a range of resources based
around the Barking Reading project (Kosky and Trickey, 1982)
and sight vocabulary teaching materials (Sigston and
Addington, 1982).   They were used to devise individual
programmes carried out by class teachers and monitored by the
special needs teacher. Information collected on children
indicated that these were effective in helping the younger
children in the school to master early reading skills.   It
was felt that amongst the third and fourth year juniors there
was a substantial number of children for whom these materials
were not yet appropriate;   their level of reading ability was
such that they were likely to encounter difficulties with the
secondary school curriculum.

Step One : Needs Analysis

The concern for this group became apparent in the course
of regular meetings between staff and members of the Schools
Psychological Service, the author and a partner specialist
reading teacher.   This led to discussions of the encouraging

results of 'home-reading' that were beginning to be reported at the time and a general view emerged that this could be a viable response.

Step Two : Clarification and Data Collection

The group of pupils causing concern was identified. This was decided by administering a group reading test and operating an arbitrary 'cut-off' to identify the 'poorest' fourth years and 17 'poorest' third years. Further baseline information on these children was collected just prior to the intervention.

Within the school, home reading was generally encouraged but there was not a school-wide policy. Cursory investigations indicated that it was almost completely absent amongst the group under scrutiny.

Step Three : Goal Setting

As the rationale for the project was that home reading would bring about the improvements of reading ability, it seemed important to ensure that there had been change in parent behaviour. We also wished the consumers to find the project beneficial. Hence the goals for the project were:

to increase the frequency of parents hearing their children read;

to produce discernible improvements in children's reading;

for parents (and children) to say that it was worth while.

Step Four : Intervention

Within the catchment area of the school, relatively few children stayed on at a secondary school beyond statutory leaving age and this was equally true of parents school careers. Teachers in similar schools often express the view that parents show a lack of interest in schooling; in reality their experiences as former pupils often have done little to encourage the strengths they have to offer. As a result they may not respond to the conventional forms of invitation made by schools on open evenings and the like. While this was certainly true for this group, nearly all parents were represented at an initial planning meeting thanks to strategies adopted by the headteacher. The initial general letter to parents made the assumption that they would be coming, asking them to return a slip to indicate which of two nights was more convenient for them. Parents who did not respond to this were sent a personal letter emphasising its importance and again asking which evening was more suitable. If these were not successful, the final approach was made personally by telephone or face to face. It is worth adding at this point that later parental reaction to the project fully justified this low level of pressure.

At the evening meetings short presentations were made by the head teacher, the author, the specialist reading teacher and a member of staff who had taken a particular interest in the area. The aims were to teach parents a simple listening technique emphasising fluent reading and swift correction of errors, build confidence in parents to carry out the activity and offer an opportunity to examine materials and ask questions. All the staff involved in the day-to-day running of the project also attended. Parents tended to be fairly passive during formal parts of the meeting but were more forthcoming when they had the chance to look at and discuss books to be read.

By the conclusion of the meetings we asked parents to enter into a 'contract' with the school for the duration of the project, which was approximately one term. The divisions of responsibility were as follows:

The parents would:

   - try to hear their children read each weekday for a period of three eggtimers (supplied if required);
   - record the number of lines read and enter a comment on the record form.

The class teacher would:

   - hear the child read three times a week and enter a comment on the record form;
   - examine the record forms daily.

The head teacher would:

   - ensure that a cumulative wall chart in the hall was filled out for the number of lines read.

The special needs teacher would:

   - ensure that children were allocated books of appropriate difficulty and interest;
   - manage changes of reading book.

Obviously home reading projects present special problems to a few parents who have literacy problems themselves, which was true in this case. Schools need to have diplomatic contingency plans worked out for this eventuality.

Step Five : Monitoring the intervention

The home reading forms completed by class teachers and parents provided a running record of occasions heard and amount read. Information collected served to assure that the system was operating as it should for most children. Where it was not, it informed a response to the problems that seemed to be inhibiting home reading taking place.

Step Six : Evaluation

The evaluation was carried out in relation to the goals set. Precise information can be found in Sigston et al (1984). Counts taken from the reading record sheets indicated that parents had heard their children very much more frequently. Testing on the Salford Sentence Reading Test (Bookbinder, 1976) just before and after the project indicated that improvements in reading accuracy were substantially greater than expected on average past progress. On an anonymous questionnaire the great majority of parents stated that their children enjoyed reading more than before the project and that they would recommend the project to other parents and schools.

It would seem that the goals set for the project had been achieved. At a more informal level, the character of the follow-up meetings, to which a parent-governor came, was quite different. Although only two-thirds attended, people spoke freely and confidently about their children's learning. Aside from the obvious endorsement of what had happened, two parents who claimed to be initially diffident volunteered that they now had a deeper understanding of the school curriculum. Another was almost accusative as to the unavailability of the project earlier in their child's career. A mother and step-father, who had experienced doubts about their ability to get their son to co-operate with the listening session, reported that he now showed his non-compliance in refusing to stop. A repeated theme that arose was that parents welcomed the **direct guidance on what to do,** as most had tried in the past but had completely given up after a number of fraught and tearful sessions.

Step Seven : From Project to Policy

One aspect of the evaluation data tended to suggest that children with lower levels of skill at the outset benefited more from higher levels of home reading, as well as being in greater need of assistance. For these reasons the school felt it was important to have a policy capable of flexibly responding to needs. The policy agreed upon was that throughout the school arrangements would be made for a set number of opportunities (according to need) to be heard reading in school and parents would be asked to match this.

Variations on a Theme

As mentioned earlier, most of the parental involvement projects in mainstream schools have centred on reading. In a comprehensive collection of practitioner-produced papers,

Topping and Wolfendale (1985) show the wide range of groups of children and settings where home reading has proved successful as well as highlighting different techniques that can be used.

Woolgar (1985) demonstrates that parents working on regular, short home assignments, can also be highly effective in improving their children's mathematical development. Gregory, Meredith and Woodward (1982) looked at a school's attempts to improve the content and attendance at a secondary school's consultation evening. Through various changes in arrangements and contents they were able considerably to increase parental attendance.

Concluding Comments

The current burgeoning of parental involvement projects has arisen from an evolving philosophy concerning the place of parents in the educational process. The increasing respect for the interests of parents in the well-being and development of their offspring has led to a gradual accumulation of rights for parents through legislation.

As well as these moral and legal pressures toward greater parental involvement there is a simple practical one: outcomes for children seem to be better from all points of view. It seems important to put parental involvement projects within this context and that of their relationship to current school policy and practice, rather than to view them as a series of "one-off" pragmatic exercises.

If parental involvement projects are to develop into longer-term significance, they must negotiate the hazards of institutional change. The management of change is deceptively difficult and protracted, presenting quite different problems from those encountered in ensuring that a static organisation is functioning efficiently. With any innovation it cannot be clear at the outset what the eventual responsibilities of participants will be. Without delineation of duties there are no sanctions that might normally be available to line managers. The role of the manager therefore rests upon building on people's strengths and facilitating the joint formulation of their duties as the project comes to fruition. Hopefully this paper provides some guidance on how to achieve this.

The staff of all institutions have their share of bitter cynics who have seen energetic innovators come and go to little effect. Overtly or by implication they will ask the question, "Why should we change?"

The need to reply satisfactorily to this places an often shirked responsibility on the manager of change to be able to demonstrate that a better state of affairs prevails as a result. The Action Research Model described seems to provide

147

a useful framework that can bridge the facilitation of change, evaluation and policy development. As such it has much to offer in the management of schools.

Chapter Ten

INVOLVING PUPILS IN THEIR OWN ASSESSMENT

Irvine Gersch

Management and the School: A Theoretical Starting Point

In recent years, educationalists have become increasingly interested in the areas of **management** and **assessment** as
applied to schools. Training courses and books on these
subjects are much in evidence, and demonstrate a growing
demand for information, and indeed, practical assistance
(Bush et al, 1980).

There are a variety of theories of management which have
developed, and which differ significantly in their conception
of the worker. These theories of management can probably be
applied to pupils as well as teachers. One of the very
earliest of these, developed at the beginning of the century,
was what has been termed "scientific management". This
approach aimed to improve efficiency by a close scientific
analysis of the task. In the 1940s, the Human Relations
approach, which viewed humans as social beings, motivated at
work by social needs, became more prevalent. This approach
stressed the importance of regarding people as humans, who
worked best when there was a genuine concern for their
well-being (Lund, 1983).

One important contribution to management theory has been
made by Douglas McGregor (1960) who described two sets of
assumptions about people at work, referred to as "Theory X"
and "Theory Y", each obviously influencing management style.
According to "Theory X", workers are seen as naturally lazy,
unambitious, and resistant to change. They dislike work and
responsibility, preferring to do as little as possible and
wishing to be led from above. The implications for management, therefore, are that managers must take responsibility
for the enterprise, workers should be controlled through
rewards, punishments or threats of punishments, and clear
direction is required. An alternative view of the worker is
contained in "Theory Y", which holds that workers are
basically able and willing to assume responsibility, ready to
work hard to achieve organisational goals, have potential for

149

development (which may have been dampened by their past experience at work), and that work is viewed as enjoyable and natural. The implication for managers, therefore, is that they need to organise things so that people can direct their own efforts, and achieve their own goals in line with organisational objectives (Handy, 1983). Clearly, whichever "theory of the worker" one has will influence one's view of managing people in organisations, and this applies to children as well as teachers.

In reality, people are probably much more complex than is indicated by the above conceptualisation, and they are undoubtedly driven by many complicated motivations, which may change over time. Nonetheless, one could ask about the assumptions head teachers, heads of year or heads of department in schools make about their staff, and additionally, what assumptions teachers make about their pupils. Are children regarded as basically lazy, work-shy, unmotivated and resistant to change, or as keen to learn and waiting for their potential to be realised? Can pupils take more responsibility for the direction of their learning, become more actively involved in decision-making in class and in school, and indeed, can teachers encourage a "self-actualisation process" whereby pupils are encouraged to be more mature, accept responsibility and develop their own potential? Undoubtedly, teachers will have their own preferences for "Theory X" or "Theory Y" in respect of their pupils.

Another important set of theories of management may be termed contingency theory or the situational approach (Handy, 1983; Gray and Starke, 1984). This approach emphasises the facts that organisations are changing and flexible, that people differ, and that effective management depends upon the situation and may need to vary according to different circumstances. For example, some workers may have a high need for security, guidance, structure and clarity, whilst others may have opposite and different needs. Furthermore, such requirements for individuals may change over time, in different circumstances, and for different tasks. One implication for managers (of staff and children) is that they will need to undertake a systematic analysis of the tasks, the resources available, and most importantly, the needs and abilities of those whom they are attempting to manage, in order to adopt the most suitable management style for each individual. This approach emphasises the complexity of the real world.

An important psychological theory which applies as much to 'management' as to pupil assessment is Kelly's Personal Construct Theory (Kelly, 1955; Bannister, 1966). This theory stresses the importance of people's attitudes or constructs when viewing the world. According to George Kelly, people behave like scientists, in that they make guesses or predictions about other people and events, which

150

they test out in reality. In the light of their results, or experience, people may or may not modify their basic views. It is as if each person has their own set of distinctive "goggles" through which they see the world. These goggles or series of goggles (technically referred to as "constructs") are individual and unique, and provide the categories whereby the world is discriminated. People negotiate the world, interpreting what is experienced, and base their perceptions on their past experiences and anticipations. Within Personal Construct Theory, people are seen as active participants and not passive recipients of external events. Each person creates his or her own experiential world, which includes events in the outside world, as well as their inner thoughts, emotions and sensations. Additionally, constructions are based upon memories, anticipations, hopes, fears and plans. In short, to understand the person one must understand his or her construction of the world and the underlying bases of those constructions (Ravenette 1977, 1980). Problems can arise when there is a mismatch between the person's own view of events and those of others. It is vital, therefore, to recognise and acknowledge that each person has their own unique and individual interpretation of the world.

The Importance of Perceptions

All that has been said so far underlines the importance of perceptions. Applied to the management of people, certain false assumptions can lead to major difficulties. Managers may take the view that their perspective of the world is the **only** one that counts, and even worse, they may think that other people view the world in the same way as themselves (Lund, 1983).

In school, Head Teachers and Heads of Department may well view things differently, junior teachers are likely to have different perceptions from Head Teachers and, certainly, children might be expected to view school life rather differently from their teachers.

Pupils' Views of Schools and Assessments

There is not a great deal of literature on the subject of pupils' views of school and assessments, despite the fact that it is always fascinating to discover what children say about their schools. One wonders whether there exist some taboos or inhibitions about seeking children's free comments, given the paucity of literature available.

However, in December 1967 the Observer newspaper invited secondary pupils to describe "the school that I'd like". The responses make interesting reading, and contain many complaints and criticisms of school life, such as comments about schools being too restrictive. The picture is drawn of schools seeming unable to free children to learn, or of pupils behaving in a passive way, receiving "knowledge" provided by teachers. For many, school is viewed as boring and the systems of discipline are seen as too prohibitive. Many of the children, however, are very positive about their teachers. Examinations are heavily criticised although interestingly, many pupils think it important to assess achievement. Essentially, children want a more active part in their learning, they want to learn to govern themselves and to be treated in a more adult way (Blishen, 1970).

In a similar survey by White and Brockington (1983), seventy young people, all of whom had left school, were invited to comment about their school experience. The results, although again not particularly representative, are of interest. Youngsters spoke of the work not always being relevant, they wanted to learn more about the "world outside", and about such subjects as marriage, divorce and life in general. The youngsters thought that examinations and qualifications mattered, and several described a sense of failure at leaving school without qualifications.

In a recent study by Lawrence, Steed and Young (1984), disruptive behaviour and episodes in school were analysed by asking pupils, as well as teachers, to describe particular incidents in some detail. This method would appear to have much to commend it. The events described demonstrate that there is a great deal of room for misinterpretation and conflict.

Docking (1980), surveying the literature, points out that anxiety-provoking situations are likely to trigger disruptive behaviour. Such issues as teachers grumbling at pupils, favouritism, reprimands seen as unfair, failure to make the work interesting, school dinners, lack of privacy in the toilets, finding the work too difficult and examinations are all sources of anxiety to pupils. Further stress factors, including grading systems, school transfers and assessment, as well as the fear of being shown up by teachers or being ridiculed, are also mentioned as potential problem areas for pupils (Docking, 1980).

Having underlined the importance of perceptions, and surveyed briefly some pupils' view of school and assessment, it is now possible to turn to pupil involvement in assessment. The next section surveys the types of assessment prevalent, the current role of pupils in such assessments and, following a critique of current practice, considers some of the arguments for and against increasing the active involvement of pupils in their assessment.

Pupil Involvement in Assessment

Types of Assessment Currently Prevalent

Children are frequently assessed these days by teachers, psychologists, doctors, speech therapists, other therapists, social workers, residential care workers and many other professional adults in a wide variety of settings.

Within schools, children are subjected to tests and examinations in order to evaluate their performance. There are tests of reading proficiency, spelling, number work, intelligence and so on. There are many text books which provide lists of tests and assessment techniques which are available to teachers (e.g., Jackson, 1968; Frith and Macintosh, 1984; Shipman, 1983; Satterly, 1981). Although there has been a move away from standardised intelligence testing, and the search for new and more appropriate ways of assessing pupil performance continues, there can be no doubt that assessment is seen as an important part of school life.

For children with special educational needs, the 1981 Education Act specifies a clear and formal procedure for the assessment of individual children. Such children are typically interviewed by psychologists who carry out tests of ability and attainment, as well as assessments of the child's attitude towards the school, home, learning, friends, and their difficulties. A curriculum-based assessment may also be carried out, whereby specific questions are asked about what the child is currently doing in relation to the curriculum, what appropriate targets might be set, and what the child might have to do to reach these targets (Ainscow and Tweddle, 1979).

Children with special needs are usually examined by doctors, given standardised tests by their teachers, and they might also be involved in family interviews conducted by social workers and psychiatrists. They may be given further tests or be assessed by speech therapists, psychotherapists, occupational therapists or medical specialists. Some children may be interviewed on their own - or with other members of the family - by a child psychiatrist or social worker attached to a Child and Family Consultation Service or Child Guidance Clinic. Indeed, the formal procedures laid down for assessing pupils under the 1981 Education Act require that local education authorities seek educational, psychological and medical advice, parent evidence and advice from other specialists, as appropriate, in order to complete their formal assessment of a child's special educational needs. (D.E.S., 1978; D.E.S. Circular 1/83).

As well as being assessed in schools, children are also assessed in Social Service establishments. Extended assessments may be carried out in observation and assessment centres, involving reports being prepared by social workers, teachers, residential care workers and other professionals.

It is probably clear from this that the word 'assessment' may mean different things to the different professionals involved, and that different detailed procedures are implied. What is certain, however, is that many professional adults are engaged in the assessment of individual children.

It is important, of course, to be clear about the aims and purposes of assessments. These can include assessing children's strengths and weaknesses, their medical or other conditions, examining their performance under specific conditions, enabling pupils to obtain formal qualifications, helping to make future plans, setting up behaviour modification programmes, deciding upon the next piece of work to be carried out, checking up what a child or group of children has learned, or generally evaluating pupil attitudes, views and styles of learning.

Conventional Role of Children in Assessment

Although the process and purpose of assessment may vary from professional to professional, and indeed there are different emphases on tests, observation and other techniques, children themselves are conventionally ascribed a subservient role in the whole assessment process. They are often expected to carry out specified tasks, answer specific questions, undertake written activities or follow set procedures. The child is generally seen as a relatively "passive object", and assessment is viewed as something which is "done to the child" rather than involving the child very actively. If one goes further and asks about children as decision-makers in school, it is arguable that children's actual choices in school tend to be very limited and artificial.

Interestingly, in the field of child care, workers have begun to take into account the views of young people and there is a growing literature designed to help professionals increase the active participation of the client (Gardner, 1985). Educationally, there are a number of interesting assessment projects in which children's views are directly sought, for example in pupil profiling (McNaughton, 1986) and the Oxford Certificate of Educational Achievement (Oxford University, 1985).

Critique of Current Practice

It is unfortunate that children are frequently assigned too passive a role in the assessment process. Indeed, if the 'subject' joins in too actively, or becomes too questioning or challenging, he or she might be regarded as interfering. Perhaps, the time-honoured idea of children "knowing their place" and "being seen and not heard" has left its mark when it comes to pupil assessments.

To be fair, many behavioural practitioners and psychologists go a long way towards involving children (and indeed parents) in decisions and plans about treatment goals, rewards, targets and so on, discussing openly with the child the purpose, nature and outcome of the assessment. Nonetheless, further advances could well be made in developing the active involvement of children in their assessments, in the variety of contexts discussed above.

Rationale for Involving Pupils more Actively in their Assessments

There are at least three main arguments for increasing the active participation of children in their assessment: pragmatic, moral and, in certain circumstances, legally supported.

1. Pragmatic: from a pragmatic point of view, children have much valuable information to contribute. Their own attitudes and ideas are likely to affect the success or otherwise of any plans or programmes drawn up for them. It is all too easy to assume that we know the child's viewpoint, and to overlook the difficulties of getting inside another person's skin. If the aim of an assessment is to work out plans for children, then the more direct the involvement of the child in the plan itself, the better the plan is likely to work out. In short, it is obviously helpful to ask the child what he or she thinks about future plans. In the school context, it makes sense to ask pupils what they regard as their strengths and weaknesses, what subjects they find hard to learn, and what help they think they need.

2. Moral: from a moral point of view, it can also be argued that children have the right to be listened to when changes in their education and schooling are going to be suggested. Clearly, listening needs to be defined in a real rather than mechanical sense. Some professionals may need to learn how to encourage children to express their views constructively, and indeed, some children may need to learn how to put across their views appropriately.

3. Legally supported: in certain circumstances, there is a legal duty to ascertain the views of children. With regard to social work practice, the Children Act (D.H.S.S., 1975) requires that "in reaching any decision relating to a child in their care, a local authority shall . . . as far as is practicable, ascertain the wishes and feelings of the child regarding the decision

155

and give due consideration to them, having regard to his age and understanding" (72, 59). This point is further emphasised by the D.H.S.S. Working Party (1981) in their consideration of the rights of the child (Sections 100-105). Educationally, D.E.S. Circular 1/83, in respect of the 1981 Education Act, states that in assessment, "the feelings and perceptions of the child concerned should be taken into account, and the concept of partnership should, wherever possible, be extended to older children and young persons" (p.2). While a D.E.S. Circular may not be legally binding, it is clear that the spirit of the law is in favour of the inclusion of children's views.

Having mounted the above three arguments, I would now like to address several counterviews which are often put forward as arguments **against** involving children actively in their own assessments.

Some Counterviews to Children being Involved in their Assessments

(i) "Children are too immature for their views to be taken seriously."

This has not been found to be the case in the author's experience. Having listened to the accounts of nursery pupils about what behaviour is and is not acceptable, and to primary school pupils talking about the specialist provision available to certain children, the impression has been gained that even young children are remarkably perceptive in their understanding of special needs, and certainly worth listening to. Of course, one has to acknowledge at all times that the views expressed are those of children and not adults.

(ii) "They might criticise their teachers and others."

Indeed, it is possible that if one invites children's views of their schooling and assessment, negative criticism might result. This raises questions about whether one should be teaching children to be able to respond in a constructively critical way, and indeed whether simply by silencing children the criticisms will go away. One could argue that it would be better to hear what children have to say, and perhaps consider modifications, rather than simply ignore comments because they might be uncomfortable.

(iii) "They won't be able to cope with the task."

Again, this has not been borne out by the author's own experience, even with quite significantly disturbed young

156

people in a Social Services Care setting.

(iv) "They will mess about."

It is clear that some children will "mess about", though the vast majority, in my experience, do not. Most pupils value being asked for their opinion, as do adults, and enjoy the experience very much. Most children report that they enjoy being treated in a mature and responsible way, and they tend to respond sensibly.

(v) "Adults have to make the decisions any way, and we should not deny 'our parental role' by abnegating the decision making to the children."

This is a relevant point. It is clearly important to distinguish the final burden of decision-making from the notion of contributing to planning. It would seem only fair to point out to children that, although their view is being sought, decisions about their future are likely to be made by adults. My own experience has been that children readily understand the distinction; they quickly accept that adults have certain responsibilities for decision-making, but they nonetheless value contributing their views to the assessment procedure.

(vi) "What about young or mentally handicapped children?"

Obviously, one has to take into account the child's ability, age and level of comprehension. It is the author's experience that mentally handicapped youngsters are able to express preferences, if choices are put to them in a simple, straightforward way. Indeed, such students have very clear and determined views about what they enjoy and do not enjoy doing. Adults may have to be creative in looking at ways of increasing the participation of slow learning children in their assessments, and it may be useful to consider involvement along a continuum, with "minimum child activity" at one end and "maximum child activity" at the other. One should thus be considering ways of gradually and increment-ally increasing the active engagement of pupils in their assessment, taking into account individual circumstances and taking care not to underestimate the child's potential.

Four Practical Projects on Pupil Involvement

In this section I intend to describe four practical projects in which I have been involved. The first describes the invention of a Child's Report, in a residential Social Services Observation and Assessment Centre; the second looks

157

at a pupil self-graded behaviour programme in a junior school class; the third involves pupil participation in a school systems change project; and the fourth deals with the inclusion of a Child's Report or Child's Advice as part of the formal assessment procedure under the 1981 Education Act for pupils with special educational needs who are the subject of 'statements'.

Project I: The Child's Report

(i) Background

Some five years ago, during a course run by the British Psychological Society, I had the opportunity to participate in a play written by the Coventry "Who Cares" group (a group of young people who have been - or are - in the care of local authorities). The children made the point that they would like to have greater involvement in their own conferences and assessments. At that time, as an educational psychologist with special responsibility for working in a local Social Services Observation and Assessment Centre, it was possible to take the idea further, and in fact to develop a Child's Report, completed by the child himself or herself, rather than by somebody else.

The Assessment Centre concerned caters for boys and girls aged between 10 and 17 years; they stay at the Centre for several months, having been referred for an extended residential assessment. The aim of the exercise is to assess the young person's needs and to plan the best course of future action, typically following a breakdown in the home circumstances. Many of the children are educated on the premises, in the Education Unit. The assessment team includes residential social work staff, education staff, a psychiatrist, an educational psychologist and a social worker, all of whom prepare reports on the child and family during the child's stay at the Centre. As in most Observation and Assessment Centres, towards the end of the child's stay all of the reports prepared are collated into a dossier or booklet and discussed in detail at a case conference, the aim being to sum up agreed suggestions about the child's future plans.

(ii) Implementation of the Child's Report

The next step in the development of the Child's Report involved detailed discussion with the Centre staff about the idea of increasing the involvement of pupils in their assessments. Several stimulating staff meetings took place, and there was open debate about the purpose of assessment, the role of children, what information could and should be shared with pupils, the misuse of 'labels' in reports, and feedback of information to children. The discussion between staff was illuminating in its own right, and challenged all of those contributing reports to be more open with the children on whom reports were being prepared. The idea of a Child's Report was agreed and a format drafted, piloted and subsequently evaluated. The Child's Report is now a permanent part of the assessment procedure at the Centre concerned.

(iii) The Child's Report

The Child's Report (which is reprinted on the following pages) is in fact a two page form, on which the children are invited to express their views under five main headings.

1. School
2. Home
3. Time at the Centre
4. Hobbies and pastimes
5. The future

The form is given to each child admitted to the Centre, and although completion is voluntary, children are encouraged to fill in as much of the form as they are able. Help is offered to them, although most usually write their answers themselves. (There was some discussion about using a blank sheet rather than having the form structured, but it was felt that the latter would be easier for children to deal with.) Children complete the form in their own handwriting, the end product being added to the booklet and placed together with all the other professional reports. It is never summarised or abridged in any way.

(iv) Evaluation of the Report.

After almost two years of use, it was decided to evaluate the report. Discussions took place with the youngsters and staff, and an evaluation questionnaire was completed by all staff and a sample of children. Although the sample of thirteen children and twenty two staff members was small and, from a statistical point of view, any results must be regarded with caution, the findings were consistent with views frequently expressed during discussion by staff and children. On the whole, the form was felt to be worthwhile and of value to staff and children. All of the children sampled had elected to complete the form. Some children felt that the report had helped them think about their future, and the majority of children said that they had answered honestly. The report seemed to encourage constructive dialogue between the child and care workers. A detailed evaluation is reported elsewhere (Gersch and Cutting, 1985).

159

CONFIDENTIAL

Child's Report by Irvine S. Gersch and M.C. Cutting
London Borough of Waltham Forest 1981

Name _____

School _____

Date _____

This is a chance for you to say what you feel about your future plans,
schooling and time at Pear Tree. The aim of this report, which you can
complete if you like, is to tell the people who are concerned with making plans about you, **your** views and ideas. Please fill in as much as
you can, leave out any sections you like, and remember that there are
no right or wrong answers.

A. School

1. What school do you attend/did you last attend?

    _____

2. How do/did you get on there?

    _____

3. What do/did you like about the school?

    _____

4. What do/did you dislike about the school?

    _____

5. Any other comments about school you wish to add?

    _____

6. Are/were there any particular teachers you got on very well with?

    _____

B. Home

1. Who is in your family?

    _____

2. What do you like doing at home?

    _____

3. What do you dislike doing at home?

    _____

4. Any comments you would like to add?

    _____

160

C. Time at Pear Tree

Do you feel that your time at Pear Tree has been useful to you?
Write here your views about your stay at Pear Tree.

_____

_____

Is there a particular person you feel you can talk easily to at Pear
Tree? If so, who?

_____

_____

D. Hobbies and Pastimes

1. What are your favourite school subjects?

_____

_____

2. What do you like doing out of school?

_____

_____

3. Do you have a particular hobby or interest? If so, what?

_____

_____

4. Who are your best friends?

_____

_____

5. What do you do mostly when you are not in school?

_____

_____

E. The Future

What do you feel should be arranged for your future? What would you
like to happen to you?

_____

_____

It is worth commenting that staff as a whole had debated the idea together and as a group felt that the idea was worth putting into action;   it could not have been introduced 'cold' without considerable risk of failure.

Project II: A self-grading behavioural programme in a junior school

(i) Pre-amble

The second project to be described concerns a behaviour modification programme in a mainstream 4th year junior class involving children tracking and grading their own progress. The project was undertaken with a whole class and devised by the author and Ms. Kate Brown (Class Teacher).

(ii) Background

As the psychologist visiting a particular mainstream school, my advice was sought about a particular child who was 'not cooperating', failing to progress, not completing work, and who generally seemed unmotivated. Such referrals are far from rare and children often respond to individual behaviour and reward programmes. One possibility was to set up a programme involving 'little tasks to complete', with the results charted and rewards made contingent upon successful completion of the task. However, for various reasons, the class teacher and myself were led into a discussion about the possibility of setting up a programme which might be of benefit to all the children in the class.

(iii) Outline of the behaviour programme for the whole class

Each child in the class was given a work record sheet which had space for 15 tasks to be completed. The descriptions of the tasks were set by the teacher on a daily basis. The child had to tick the next column when the task had been completed and then give himself or herself a grade for work effort.   Initially, a four point scale was utilised as follows:-

A = excellent effort
B = good effort
C = satisfactory effort
D = not very good effort

The teacher then wrote in her grade, along the same scale, in discussion with the child. Finally, points were allocated, in the final column, according to the teacher's grading (A = 3 points, B = 2 points, C = 1 point, D = 0 points). The points were added up at the end of the week, and each point earned one minute of free time (indoor games, free choice activity or going to help in another class). The charts were signed by the class teacher and head teacher and were taken home every week. There is little doubt that parental involvement in such programmes can provide immense motivation for children, and that such parental power is often underrated.

(iv) Features of the system

Several features of the behavioural programme, which clearly involves pupils in assessing their performance are of note:

1. It encourages children to develop organisational skills and to begin to think about their work effort, self-critically.
2. It encourages pupils to assess their own efforts and to compare their own perceptions with those of the teachers, who in turn are encouraged to make explicit to children the criteria of success.
3. Children receive more frequent and more immediate feedback about their work than is usual.
4. The system encourages children to begin to take a greater responsibility for their own work.
5. Work tasks can be broken down into small, manageable chunks.
6. Over a period of time, children can learn to predict teacher reaction more accurately, and indeed vice versa. Teachers may learn much about what children expect of themselves and their work. The process encourages two-way negotiation and understanding.

(v) Evaluation

In order to evaluate the system, all the children in the class were given a questionnaire to complete, classroom discussions took place, parents were given a quesionnaire and the teacher was interviewed. The following major findings emerged:

1. 94% of pupils enjoyed the system.
2. 56% of pupils said that they were putting more effort into their work.
3. 44% of pupils said that they agreed with the teacher grades, the rest felt that the teacher's grades were 'too low' and, just occasionally and to a lesser extent, 'too high'.
4. All the children were pleased to earn free time and listed their preferred (rewarding) activities as playing, watching TV or video, drawing, chalking on the board,

163

chatting and, interestingly, helping in another class with younger pupils.

5. The children suggested a finer scale of points (that is a 5 point scale), so that small increments of effort could be detected and recorded. Not surprisingly, they also suggested that there should be more opportunities for earning free time rewards.

6. Only a few parents replied to the evaluation question- naire and letter, but all those who responded did so favourably, saying that they liked the idea of the reward system.

The teacher herself made several comments about the system. She thought that:-

1. Children were learning to be more self-disciplined.

2. The grades given by teacher and pupils were becoming closer, as time went on, and the system had encouraged her to think carefully about the criteria for her grading.

3. Pupil effort has improved to some extent, but not necess- arily consistently; many of the pupils in the class were working hard any way.

4. The system was felt to be viable, in the classroom, but its organisation had to be carefully considered and planned.

5. The fact that the report was sent home to parents was seen to be of particular merit and important to children.

6. The teacher regarded the system as worthwhile and wished to continue using it. She noted that other teachers in the school have shown an interest in utilising the system.

The original system was revised in the light of the evaluation exercise, and now contains a five point scale and more opportunities for rewards.

Project III: Pupil Participation in a School's System Change

During a project carried out in a secondary school (Gersch, 1984), the author worked with a whole secondary school staff in order to attempt to improve control and discipline within the school. Following full staff meeting and paper given to the school staff on current research, a working party was set up to investigate the rules, rewards and sanctions currently employed in school and to suggest improvements which might be possible in the school.

Over a period of about two years various changes occurred within the school; in particular, three main sub-systems of the school were altered in respect of:

      a. The school rules.
      b. The merit or reward system.
      c. The sanction system.

With regard to the school rules, the present school rules, which were not well known by all staff, were discussed, and research was carried out on the children's attitudes to the rules which were felt to be important. A new set of very carefully worded rules was drafted after debate, and became the substance of further discussion with children. The rules were included in the staff and children's handbook and used as a basis for form tutors to discuss regularly with their pupils.

    It seems important to stress that the children's involvement in rule making was found to be particularly helpful and, interestingly enough, the children tended to vote for "protective rules" in which they were themselves protected from other children interfering with them or hurting them in any way. Most children accepted the need for general school rules.

    The second sub-system which was set up was a merit or reward system. A survey of staff and children revealed that too few rewards were being employed in school and, when pupils' views were sought, it was found that letters home would be a potent reinforcer for children. A merit system involving teachers giving out points to children, with points being exchangeable for merit certificates to be sent home, proved to be a most valuable innovation. Here again, it was of interest that it was found important to involve the children in the selection of preferred rewards. It is all too easy to assume that we know in advance what rewards are likely to be favoured by children, and often errors can be made.

Project IV: Reassessment of Thirteen-Year-Old Pupils Under the 1981 Education Act

    The 1981 Education Act requires, amongst other things, that local authorities reassess thirteen-year-old pupils, in order to provide a fresh statement of their special educational needs. Given the maturity level of thirteen-year-old pupils, and the fact that the implicit aim of the assessment is to help prepare the child for leaving school and for the final stage of school, it was felt desirable to attempt to increase the involvement of pupils in their assessments.

    In Waltham Forest, it was decided to extend the Child's Report described earlier and to produce a format which could be utilised by thirteen-year-old pupils with special educational needs. Pupils are given a report which they may complete in order to state their views about their schooling and special needs, and which is to become part of their legal 'statement' of special educational needs (added to the other professional reports).

The report invites children to answer questions under the following headings:-

A. School background
B. Present school
C. Special needs
D. Friends
E. Hobbies, interests and out of school activities
F. The future
G. Additional comments

Although we are still in the early stages of developing formal "Child's Advice" as part of the assessment procedures under the 1981 Education Act, so far we have found that:-

(i) children enjoy and value the experience of being consulted;

(ii) children say sensible and interesting things;

(iii) many children are extremely perceptive about their schooling;

(iv) some parents have requested that their children complete a report when placements have been controversial;

(v) guidelines and training are probably required for adult helpers, and care is needed not to bias children. Pupils may be unused to expressing themselves freely, and may need support to do so;

(vi) some children have found the actual form piloted rather too hard to complete and we shall probably have to devise parallel versions for children in different educational settings;

(vii) some children experience a status boost and a sense of importance, feeling that they are being treated in a mature and responsible way.

A Model for Increasing the Active Involvement of Pupils in their Assessments

In this section, it is intended to raise some questions for assessors and teachers, and then to suggest one possible model for increasing the active involvement of pupils in assessment. As said earlier, children currently participate in assessments to some degree, but the thesis of this chapter is that it may be possible to increase the active involvement of some children in the assessment process. It might be helpful to consider the degree of pupil involvement at present and to enquire whether a greater degree of involvement is possible along a hypothetical continuum from 'minimal involvement' to a 'high degree of involvement'.

```
0     1     2     3     4     5     6     7     8     9    10

minimal pupil        moderate          reasonably        high degree
involvement          pupil             active            of pupil
                     involvement       pupil             involvement
                                       involvement
```

Figure VII   Continuum indicating the degree of pupil involvement

The following sorts of questions might well be posed as a starting point:-

1. How is the child's view to be sought?
2. What does the child think the assessment is for?
3. What does the child think constitutes appropriate/ inappropriate, desirable/undesirable responses?
4. How do other adults view the child's role in the assessment process?
5. How is the child to be introduced to and prepared for the assessment?
6. How is the information gained to be fed back to the child?
7. To what degree is the child presently involved in the assessment process (see above continuum)?
8. Is the child's ability to respond or comprehend being under-estimated?
9. Could the child be more actively involved?
10. What would the child like to learn, to change or to come out of the assessment?

There are clearly other questions which could be asked along the same lines.

Some Further Possibilities for Involving Pupils

Although several projects have been discussed above, there does appear to be considerable scope for increasing the active involvement of pupils in their schooling. In this section it is intended only to pinpoint some areas worthy of further consideration.

a) Dealing with disruptive behaviour

Whenever behaviour problems occur between pupils and

167

teachers, it may be expected that at least two points of view or explanations will arise. The work of Lawrence, Steed and Young (1984) emphasises the importance of analysing problems in as wide a context as possible. All too often we do not listen sufficiently to what children have to say about disruptive events, triggers to such events, and the meaning of such behaviour to them. In short, what is being advocated is a policy of inviting children to discuss their perception of disruptive behaviour more openly when problems arise.

b) Evaluation of lessons, teaching material and teaching methods

In the Open University there is now a vast body of knowledge in respect of student behaviour which has been built up systematically by seeking student feedback about the University's texts, materials, complexity of tasks given, clarity and so on. Material is revised and indeed improved in the light of student feedback (Gibbs 1985).

It is interesting that we rarely ask pupils for their feedback in respect of lessons, materials presented by teachers and styles of presentation. What is being advocated is encouragement for teachers to invite pupils to provide constructive criticism of lessons and learning tasks, and that pupils be encouraged to learn ways of providing constructive, mature feedback which is free from emotional, personal or hurtful comments.

c) Pupil councils

Many schools now have pupil councils which consist of pupils, elected by their peers, who meet together in order to suggest ideas for improving the school environment, arrangements and events for pupils, and even school rules. Such councils clearly offer pupils the opportunity to learn about decision-making, to use democratic methods and to take responsibility for their school. Questions can of course arise about how far children's views are really listened to and make a difference, but nonetheless pupil councils would seem to be a useful step forward in increasing the pupil involvement in their school life.

d) Pupil profiling

The D.E.S. has made available several grants for projects on pupil profiling, which are currently in train. Such projects aim to encourage pupils to keep their own progress records and lists of their achievements.

Although such projects are in their early stages, it is
clear that pupils themselves are keen to keep their own
achievement records, they are proud of them and they are
motivated by them (McNaughton, 1986).

e) Teaching children to make decisions

During their school lives children are involved with some
decision-making, in consultation with their parents, but
it is my view that such opportunities are limited.   At
the nursery stage, children may be encouraged to choose
different activities, a process which continues through
to the infant and junior schools.   At secondary level,
they may be invited to participate in the decision about
the choice of secondary school, although for many such
decisions may be largely predetermined.   During their
secondary school career, pupils may have to decide to
'drop' subjects and indeed, essentially, secondary school
choices frequently involve negative decisions in which
children have to opt out of things, so that by the sixth
form, pupils are studying fewer and fewer subjects.   The
new GCSE will go some way to countering such negative
decisions, in that pupils will probably be studying more
subjects.

Apart from the lack of opportunities we offer children to
make decisions, perhaps more importantly we do not
actually teach them about the task of decision-making.
What is being advocated here is that decision-making
theory and practice should play a more explicit part in
the school curriculum.   Similarly, it is my view that
children need much more direct advice and guidance on
study skills, managing their own learning, tracking their
own progress and modifying their own behaviour.   In
short, it would be useful to view children as 'active
learners' who need to know about psychology, learning
theory, learning processes and the mechanics of learning.

Conclusion

It has been argued in this chapter that children should
play a more active role in their assessments and indeed in
their learning and school life.   Some practical projects on
the topic have been described and a possible model for
increasing the involvement of pupils in assessments has been
outlined.
The 1981 Education Act offers interesting opportunities
for including children's views, and a Child's Report (completed by the child himself or herself) may well be a useful
vehicle for encouraging pupil participation.

169

Certainly, creative approaches will be required if we are to succeed in increasing the active involvement of pupils in their assessments, bearing in mind individual differences and circumstances, but if we are to avoid leaving out the views of the most important person from the assessment process, the effort would seem to be most worthwhile.

Acknowledgements

I would like to acknowledge the help and support of the children, teachers, head teachers, education officers and social services staff who collaborated with the projects described in this chapter. The views expressed, however, remain the responsibility of the author, and do not necessarily reflect the policy of the L.E.A. in which the projects took place.

REFERENCES

ADELMAN, C. (1978) Action Research. In Hegarty, S. and
    Evans, P. (eds.) Research and Evaluation in Special
    Education. Windsor: N.F.E.R./Nelson
AINSCOW, M. (1984) Curriculum development in special schools.
    In Bowers, T. (ed.) Management and the Special School.
    London: Croom Helm
AINSCOW, M., and TWEDDLE, D.A. (1979) Preventing Classroom
    Failure: An Objectives Approach. Chichester: Wiley
AINSCOW, M., BOND, J., GARDNER, J. and TWEDDLE, D. (1978) A
    new role for the special school? Special Education:
    Forward Trends 5, 1, 15-16
AINSCOW, M. and MUNCEY, J. (1985) SNAP - What have we learned
    so far? Occasional Publication No.4. Coventry L.E.A.
ARGYLE, M. (1967) The Psychology of Interpersonal Behaviour.
    Harmondsworth: Penguin
ARGYRIS, C. (1970) Intervention Theory and Method. New York:
    Addison Wesley
BAILEY, T.J. (1981) The secondary remedial teacher's role
    redefined. Remedial Education 16, 132-136
BANDURA, A. (1977) Social Learning Theory. Englewood Cliffs,
    New Jersey: Prentice-Hall
BANNISTER, D. (1966) A New Theory of Personality. In Foss,
    B.M. (ed.) New Horizons in Psychology.
    Harmondsworth: Penguin
BARRETT, R.S. (1966) The influence of the supervisor's
    requirements on ratings. Personnel Psychology 19,
    375-387
BARRETT, S. and HILL, M. (1984) Policy, bargaining and
    structure in implementation theory : towards an inte-
    grated perspective. Policy and Politics 12, 219-240
BASSETT, G.A. and MEYER, H.H. (1968) Performance appraisal
    based on self-review. Personnel Psychology 21, 421-430
BAYNE, R. (1982) Interviewing. In Davey, D.M. and Harris, M.
    (eds.) Judging People. London: McGraw-Hill
BENNIS, W.G., CHIN, R. and COREY, K.E. (eds.) (1969) The
    Planning of Change. New York: Holt, Rinehart and

171

Winston

BERNE, E. (1964) Games People Play. New York: Grove

BINES, H. (1986) Redefining Remedial Education. London: Croom Helm

BLISEN, E. (ed.) (1970) The School that I'd Like. Harmondsworth: Penguin

BOLAM, R. (1975) The management of educational change. In Houghton, V., McHugh, R. and Morgan, C. (eds.) Management in Education. London: Ward Lock

BOOKBINDER, G.E. (1976) The Salford Sentence Reading Test. London: Hodder and Stoughton

BOOTH, T. and POTTS, P. (eds.) (1983) Integrating Special Education. Oxford: Blackwell

BOWERS, T. (1980) Training teachers as managers. Special Education : Forward Trends 7, 4, 31-33

BOWERS, T. (1984) Power and conflict: facts of life. In Bowers, T. (ed.) Management and the Special School. London: Croom Helm

BOWERS, T. (1984a) Introduction. In Bowers, T. (ed.) Management and the Special School. London: Croom Helm

BOWERS, T. (1987) Management and Special Needs: Case Studies in Decison-Making. Cambridge: People in Perspective

BURDEN, R. (1981) Systems theory and its relevance to schools. In Gillham, B. (ed.) Problem Behaviour in the Secondary School. London: Croom Helm

BUSH, A., GLATTER, R., GOODEY, J. and RICHES, A. (1980) Approaches to School Management. London: Harper and Row

CASHDAN, A. and PUMFREY, P. (1969) Some effects of remedial teaching of reading. Educational Research 11, 2, 138-142

CASIO, W.F. (1982) Applied Psychology in Personnel Management. Virginia: Reston

CASTEEL, V. (1984) Special needs and school-focused in-service education. In Bowers, T. (ed.) Management and the Special School. London: Croom Helm

CHAPMAN, D.W. and LOWTHER, M.A. (1982) Teachers' satisfaction with teaching. Journal of Educational Research. 75, 241-247

CHAZAN, M. (1967) The effects of remedial teaching of reading: A review of research. Remedial Education 2, 4-12

CHILDREN ACT (1975) London: H.M.S.O.

CLUNIES-ROSS, L. and WIMHURST, S. (1983) The Right Balance. Windsor: N.F.E.R./Nelson

COCKERILL, E. (1953) The interdependence of the professions in helping people. Social Casework 34, 371-378

CROLL, P. and MOSES, D. (1985) One in Five - The Assessment and Incidence of Special Educational Needs. London: Routledge and Kegan Paul

CULLEN, C. and WRIGHT, T. (1978) Selling: the social con-
structional approach applied to psychology. Bulletin of
the British Psychology Society 31, 292-294

CUNNINGHAM, W.G. (1982) Teacher burnout: Stylish fad or
proved problem? Planning and Changing 12, 219-244

DALY, B., ADDINGTON, J., KERFOOT, S. and SIGSTON, A. (eds.)
(1985) Portage: The Importance of Parents. Windsor:
N.F.E.R./Nelson

DAVIES, B. (1977) Consultancy - some of the issues. British
Journal of Inservice Education 3, 112-115

DAVIS, G. (1980) The role of the support services in helping
low achievers in the secondary school. In Raybould,
E.C., Roberts, B. and Wedell, K. (eds.) Helping the Low
Achiever in the Secondary School. Birmingham: University of Birmingham

D.E.S. (1967) Children and their Primary Schools. (The
Plowden Report). London: H.M.S.O.

D.E.S. (1977) The New Partnership for our Schools. (The
Taylor Report). London: H.M.S.O.

D.E.S. (1978) Special Educations Needs. (The Warnock
Report). London: H.M.S.O.

D.E.S. (1981) The Education Act. London: H.M.S.O.

D.E.S. (1983) The In-service Teacher Training Grants Scheme
(Circular 3/83) London: D.E.S.

D.E.S. (1984) Initial Teacher Training: Approval of Courses.
(Circular 3/84 Annex.) London: D.E.S.

D.E.S. (1984) The In-service Teacher Training Grants Scheme.
(Circular 4/84) London: D.E.S.

D.E.S. (1984) Slow Learning and Less Successful Pupils in
Secondary Schools. London: H.M.S.O.

D.E.S. (1985) The In-service Teachers Grants Scheme.
(Circular 3/85) London: D.E.S.

D.E.S. and D.H.S.S. (1983) Assessments and Statements of
Special Educational Needs. (Circulars 1/83 and HC
83/3). London: D.E.S.

DESSENT, T. (1984) Special schools and the mainstream - the
resource stretch. In Bowers, T. (ed.) Management and
the Special School. London: Croom Helm

D.H.S.S. (1981) Observation and Assessment. Report of a
Working Party. London: H.M.S.O.

DOCKING, J.W. (1980) Control and Discipline in Schools:
Perspectives and Approaches. London: Harper and Row

DOWNS, S., FARR, R.M. and COLBECK, L. (1978) Self-appraisal:
A convergence of selection and guidance. Journal of
Occupational Psychology 51, 271-278

DRUCKER, P. (1954) The Practice of Management. New York:
Harper

DUBIN, S. (1972) Obsolescence or lifelong education: A
choice for the professional. American Psychologist 27,
486-498

DUNHAM, J. (1984) Stress in Teaching. London: Croom Helm

References

EASTON, D. (1979) A Systems Analysis of Political Life. Chicago: University of Chicago Press
EDUCATION (Special Educational Needs) REGULATIONS (1983) London: H.M.S.O.
EDWARDS, C. (1985) On launching a support service. British Journal of Special Education 12, 2, 53-54
EGAN, G. (1975) The Skilled Helper: A Model for Systematic Helping and Interpersonal Relating. Monterey: Brooks Cole
EGAN, G. (1978) Change Agent Skills. Monterey: Brooks Cole
ETZIONI, A. (1976) A Comparative Analysis of Complex Organisations. New York: Free Press
FARBER, B.A. (1984) Teacher burnout: Assumptions, myths and issues. Teachers College Record 86, 321-338
FERGUSON, N. and ADAMS, M. (1982) Assessing the advantages of team teaching in remedial education: The remedial teacher's role. Remedial Education 17, 1, 24-30
F.E.U. (1981) Vocational Preparation. London: F.E.U.
F.E.U. (1982) Skills for Living. London: F.E.U.
F.E.U. (1986) A College Guide: Students with Special Needs in Further Education. London: F.E.U./Longmans
F.E.U. (In progress) Transition to Adulthood: RP95. London: F.E.U.
F.E.U./N.F.E.R. (1985) From Coping to Confidence. London: F.E.U.
F.E.U./S.C.D.C. (1985) Supporting T.V.E.I. London: F.E.U.
FISH, J. (Chairman) (1985) Equal Opportunities for all? London: I.L.E.A.
FISH, J. (1985) Special Education - The Way Ahead. Milton Keynes: Open University.
FLETCHER, C. (1982) Assessment centres. In Davey, D.M. and Harris, M. (eds.) Judging People. London: McGraw-Hill
FORMAN, S.G. and CECIL, M.A. (1985) Stress management. In Maher, C.A. (ed.) Professional Self-Management: Techniques for Special Services Providers. Baltimore: Brookes
FORSYTH, D.R. (1980) The function of attributions. Social Psychology Quarterly 43, 184-189
FRIED, Y., KENDRITH, M. and FERRIS, G.R. (1984) The physiological measurement of work stress: A critique. Personnel Psychology 37, 583-615
FRITH, D.S. and MACINTOSH, H.G. (1984) A Teacher's Guide to Assessment. Cheltenham: Stanley Thornes
FULLAN, M. (1982) The Meaning of Educational Change. Ontario: OISE
GAINS, C. (1985) Remedial education: The challenge for trainers. In Smith, C. (ed.) New Directions in Remedial Education. London: Falmer
GAINS, C.W. and McNICHOLAS (1979) Remedial Education: Guidelines for the Future. Harlow: Longman
GALLOWAY, D.M. (1985) Schools, Pupils and Special Educational

Needs.   London: Croom Helm
GARDNER, R. (1985) Client participation in decision-making in
    child care: A review of research.   Highlight   No.71
    National Children Bureau
GARNETT, J. (1983) Providing access to the mainstream
    curriculum in secondary schools.   In Booth, T. and
    Potts, P. (eds.)   Integrating Special Education.
    Oxford: Blackwell
GEORGIADES, N.J. and PHILLIMORE, L. (1975) The Myth of the
    hero-innovator and alternative strategies for organ-
    isation of change.   In Kiernan, C.C. and Woodford, F.P.
    (eds.)   Behaviour Modification with the Severely
    Retarded.   Amsterdam: Associated Scientific
GERSCH, I.S. (1984) Behaviour modification and systems
    analysis in a secondary school: Combining two
    approaches.   Behavioural Approaches with Children 8,
    83-91
GERSCH, I.S. and CUTTING, M.C. (1985) The Child's Report.
    Educational Psychology in Practice 1, 63-69
GIBBS, G. (1985) Teaching Students to Learn: A Student-
    centred Approach. Milton Keynes: Open University Press
GILLHAM, W. (1978) Reconstructing Educational Psychology.
    London: Croom Helm
GILLHAM, W. (1981) (ed.) Problem Behaviour in the Secondary
    School.   London: Croom Helm
GOLBY, M. and GULLIVER, J.R. (1979) Whose remedies, whose
    ills? A critical review of remedial education. Journal
    of Curriculum Studies 11, 137-47
GRAY, H.L. (1975) Exchange and conflict in the school. In
    Houghton, V., McHugh, R. and Morgan, C. (eds.) Manage-
    ment in Education. London: Ward Lock
GRAY, J.L. and STARKE, F.A. (1984) Organisational Behaviour.
    Columbus (Ohio): Merrill
GREEN, F. and McGINTY, J. (1979) The Curriculum: Its import-
    ance and implications.   In Dixon, K. and Hutchinson, D.
    (eds.) Further Education for Handicapped Students.
    Bolton: Bolton College of Education
GREGORY, P., MEREDITH, P. and WOODWARD, A. (1982) Parental
    involvement in a secondary school.   Journal of the
    Association of Educational Psychologists 5, 54-60
GULLIFORD, R. (1979) Remedial Work Across the Curriculum:
    Guidelines for the Future. Harlow: Longman
HANDY, C.B. (1983) Understanding Organisations.   Harmonds-
    worth: Penguin
HARGREAVES, D.H. (1972) Interpersonal Relationships and
    Education. London: Routledge and Kegan Paul
HARTLEY, C.J. (1986) Parents as partners, not puppets.
    Contact 47, 9-12
HARTLEY, J. and KELLEY, J. (1986) Psychology and industrial
    relations: from conflict to cooperation?   Journal of
    Occupational Psychology 59, 161-176

HEGARTY, S., POCKLINGTON, K. and LUCAS, D. (1981) Educating Pupils with Special Needs in the Ordinary School. Windsor: N.F.E.R./Nelson

HEGARTY, S., POCKLINGTON, K. and LUCAS, D. (1982) Integration in Action. Windsor: N.F.E.R./NELSON

HEGARTY, S., MOSES, D. and JOWETT, S. (1986) Meeting special educational needs - support for the ordinary school. N.F.E.R. Research Project Report

HERON, J. (1975) Six Category Intervention Analysis. Human Potential Research Project: University of Surrey

HOCKLEY, L. (1985) On being a support teacher. British Journal of Special Education 12, 1, 27-29

HODSON, A., CLUNIES-ROSS and HEGARTY, S. (1984) Learning Together: Teaching Pupils with Special Needs in the Ordinary School. Windsor: N.F.E.R./Nelson

HOMANS, G.C. (1958) Social behaviour and exchange. American Journal of Sociology 63, 597-606

HOPKINS, D. (1986) The change process and leadership in schools. School Organisation 6, 1, 81-100

HOWELL, W.C. and DIPBOYE, R.L. (1982) Essentials of Industrial and Organisational Psychology. Homewood, Illinois: Dorsey

HOYLE, E. (1975) Professisonality, professionalism and control in teaching. In Houghton, V., McHugh, R. and Morgan, C. (eds.) Management in Education. London: Ward Lock Educational

HOYLE, E. (1976) Strategies of curriculum change. Unit 23, Open University Course 203. Curriculum Design and Development. Milton Keynes: Open University Press

HUNTER, J.E. and HUNTER, R.F. (1984) Validity and utility of alternative predictors of job performance. Psychological Bulletin 96, 72-98

HUTCHINSON, D. (1985) Co-operation and co-ordination: Module seven of From Coping to Confidence. London: D.E.S./-F.E.U.

INDUSTRIAL SOCIETY (1964) Methods of Training your Staff. London: Industrial Society

JACKSON, S. (1968) A Teacher's Guide to Tests and Testing. Harlow: Longman

JEFFS, A. (1984) Teachers with special needs: staff development in the remedial service. Remedial Education 19, 3, 107-112

JEFFS, S. (1986) Servicing the support services. Support for Learning 1, 13-17

JINKS, M. (1979) Training. Poole: Blandford

JOHNSON, D. (1980) Crossing the boundary. In Bush, T., Glatter, R., Goodey, J. and Riches, C. (eds.) Approaches to School Management. London: Harper and Row

JOINT BOARD FOR PREVOCATIONAL EDUCATION (1984) The Certificate of PreVocational Education (C.P.V.E.) London: Joint Board

KATZ, D. and KAHN, R. (1966) The Social Psychology of Organisations. New York: Wiley

KELLY, G.A. (1955) The Psychology of Personal Constructs. New York: Norton

KENT, A.J. (1986) Educating for special needs. Handicapped Living June 1986, 30-31

KIRCHNER, W.K. and DUNNETTE, M.D. Identifying the critical factors in successful salesmanship. Personnel (September-October) 54-59

KNIGHT, R. and BOWERS, T. (1984) Developing effective teams. In Bowers, T. (ed.) Management and the Special School. London: Croom Helm

KOSKY, R. and TRICKEY, G. (1982) The Barking Project. Remedial Education 18, 53-58

LASKIER (1985) The changing role of the remedial teacher. In Smith, C. (ed.) New Directions in Remedial Education. London: Falmer

LATHAM, G.P. and WEXLEY, K.N. (1982) Increasing Productivity Through Performance Appraisal. Reading, Massachusetts: Addison-Wesley

LAWRENCE, J., STEED, D. and YOUNG, P. (1984) Disruptive Children - Disruptive Schools? London: Croom Helm

LIEBERMAN, A. (1986) Collaborative research: Working with, not working on. Educational Leadership 43, 28-32

LINDSAY, G. (1983) Problems of Adolescence in the Secondary School. London: Croom Helm

LIPPIT, R., HOOYMAN, G., SASHKIN, M. and KAPLAN, J. (1978) Resource Book for Planned Change. Ann Arbor, Michigan: Human Resource Development Associates

LOVELL, K., BYRNE, C. and RICHARDSON, B. (1963) A further study of educational progress of children who had received remedial education. British Journal of Educational Psychology 33, 3-9

LOVELL, K., JOHNSON, E. and PLATTS, D. (1962) A summary of a study of the reading ages of children who had been given remedial teaching. British Journal of Educational Psychology 32, 66-71

LUND, B. and the P670 COURSE TEAM (1983) The Effective Manager, Books 1, 4, 8. Milton Keynes: Open University

McCALL, C. (1980) Ways of providing for the low achiever in the secondary school: suggested advantages, disadvantages and alternatives. In Raybould, E.C., Roberts, B. and Wedell, K. (eds.) Helping the Low Achiever in the Secondary School. Birmingham: University of Birmingham

McCORMICK, E.J. (1979) Job Analysis: Methods and Applications. New York: AMACOM

McCORMICK and TIFFIN (1975) Industrial Psychology. London: Allen and Unwin

McGREGOR, D. (1960) The Human Side of Enterprise. New York: McGraw-Hill

177

References

McHENRY, R. (1981) The selection interview. In Argyle, M. (ed.) Social Skills and Work. London: Methuen

McNAUGHTON, J. (1986) Records of Achievement Project (Pamphlets, Project Bulletin and Personal Recording Tutors' Handbook). Chelmsford: Essex County Council

MALE, J. and THOMPSON, C. (1985) The Educational Implications of Disability - A Guide for Teachers. London: RADAR

MARGULIES, N. and WALLACE, J. (1983) Organisational Change. New York: Scott Foresman

MARKS, I. (1983) Staff Development. Times Educational Supplement 11.11.83

MARRA, M. (1984) Parents of children with moderate learning difficulties. In Bowers, T. (ed.) Management and the Special School. London: Croom Helm

MARSHALL, J. and COOPER, C.L. (1979) Executive Under Pressure: A Psychological Study. London: Macmillan

MEIER, S.T. (1984) The construct validity of burnout. Journal of Occupational Psychology 57, 211-220

MITTLER, P. (1986) Foreword. In Coupe, J. and Porter, J. (eds.) The Education of Children with Severe Learning Difficulties. London: Croom Helm

MOORE, J. (1986) Innovations from Kent. Special Children 5, 29

MORRISON, A. and McINTYRE, D. (1969) Teachers and Teaching. Harmondsworth: Penguin

N.A.C.E.D.P. (1985) The Additional Employment Problems of Young Disabled People. London: Department of Employment

N.A.R.E (1985) Guidelines 6 : Teaching Roles for Special Educational Needs. Stafford: N.A.R.E. Publications

N.A.T.F.H.E. (1983) Handicap, Disability and Special Learning Needs : A Guide to Good Practice in F.H.E. London: N.A.T.F.H.E.

N.B.H.S. (1986) Burnham: The Biggest Barrier of All. London: N.B.H.S.

NICHOLS, A. (1983) Managing Educational Innovations. London: Unwin

NOLTE, M.C. (ed.) (1966) An Introduction to Schools Administration : Selected Readings. London: Macmillan

N.U.T. (1984) Meeting Special Educational Needs in Ordinary Schools. London: N.U.T.

O'HAGEN, F.J. (1977) The role of the remedial teachers: problems and perspectives. Remedial Education 12, 56-59

OLDROYD, D., SMITH, K. and LEE, J. (1984) School-based Staff Development Activities. Harlow: Longman

OXFORD UNIVERSITY - Delagacy of Local Examinations (1985) Oxford Certificate of Educational Achievement (O.C.E.A.): Provisional Handbook and Newsletters. Oxford: University of Oxford

PAYNE, M. (1982) Working in Teams. London: Macmillan

PETERS, T.J. and WATERMAN, R.H. (1982) In Search of

Excellence: Lessons from America's Best-Run Companies. New York: Harper and Row

POPPLETON, S.E. (1981) The social skills of selling. In Argyle, M. (ed.) Social Skills and Work. London: Methuen

POPPLETON, S.E. and LUBBOCK, J. (1977) Marketing aspects of life assurance selling. European Journal of Marketing 11, 418-431

QUICKE, J. (1982) The Cautious Expert. Milton Keynes: Open University Press

RANDELL and SHAW (1972) Staff Appraisal. London: Institute of Personnel Management

RAVENETTE, A.T. (1977) Personal Construct Theory: An approach to the psychological investigation of children and young people. In Bannister, D. (ed.) New Perspectives in Personal Construct Theory. London: Wiley

RAVENETTE, A.T. (1980) The exploration of consciousness: Personal construct intervention with children. In Landfield, A.W. and Leitner, L.M. (eds.) Personal Construct Psychology : Psychotherapy and Personality London: Wiley

REYNOLDS, H. and TRAMEL, M.E. (1979) Executive Time Management. Farnborough: Gower

ROBERTSON, I.T. and MAKIN, P. (1986) Management and selection in Britain: A survey and critique. Journal of Occupational Psychology 59, 45-58

ROGERS, C. (1951) Client-Centered Therapy. Boston: Houghton Mifflin

ROSENFIELD, S. (1985) Professional development management. In Maher, C.A. (ed.) Professional Self-Management: Techniques for Special Services Providers. Baltimore: Brookes

SATTERLEY, D. (1981) Assessment in Schools. Oxford: Blackwell

SAYER, J. (1985) A whole school approach to meeting all needs. In Sayer, J. and Jones, N. (eds.) Teacher Training and Special Educational Needs. London: Croom Helm

SAYER, J. and JONES, N. (1985) Teacher Training and Special Educational Needs. London: Croom Helm.

SEWELL, G. (1982) Reshaping Remedial Education. London : Croom Helm

SEXTON, M. and SWITZER, K.D. (1978) The time management ladder. Educational Leadership 35, 482-486

SHIPMAN, M. (1983) Assessment in Primary and Middle Schools. London: Croom Helm

SIDNEY, E., BROWN, M. and ARGYLE, M. (1973) Skills with People. London: Hutchinson

SIGSTON, A. and ADDINGTON, J. (1982) Starter Pack. Barking and Dagenham Schools Psychological Service

SIGSTON, A., ADDINGTON, J., BANKS, V. and STRIESOW, M. (1984)

Progress with parents: An account and evaluation of a home reading project for poor readers. Remedial Education 19, 170-3

SMITH, C.J. (1982) Helping colleagues cope - a consultant role for the remedial teacher. Remedial Education 17, 75-78

SMITH, P.C. and KENDALL, L.M. (1963) Retranslation of expectations: An approach to the construction of unambiguous anchors for rating scales. Journal of Applied Psychology 47, 149-155

SMITH, T. (1980) Parents and Pre-School. London: Grant McIntyre

TATTUM, D. (1986) (ed.) Management of Disruptive Pupil Behaviour. Chichester: Wiley

TAYLOR, B. (1978) Wanted - a sense of direction. Times Educational Supplement 6th. Feb., p.4

TIZARD, J. (1976) Psychology and social policy. Bulletin of the British Psychological Society 29, 225-234

TIZARD, J., SCHOFIELD, W.N. and HEWISON, J. (1982) Collaboration between teachers and parents in assisting children's reading. British Journal of Educational Psychology 52, 1-15

THOMAS, G. (1986) Integrating personnel in order to integrate children. Support for Learning 1,1, 19-25

THOMAS, G. and JACKSON, B. (1986) The whole school approach to integration. British Journal of Special Education. 13, 1, 27-29

TOPPING, K. (1983) Educational Systems for Disruptive Adolescents. London: Croom Helm

TOPPING, K. and WOLFENDALE, S. (eds.) (1985) Parental Involvement in Children's Reading. London : Croom Helm

TRETHOWAN, D. (1985) . . . to appraise teachers, not to bury them. Times Educational Supplement 8.3.85

TURNER, C. (1974) Managing Change. Bristol: Resources Group, Coombe Lodge

VERNON, P.E. (1964) Personality Assessment. London: Methuen

WARNOCK, M. (Chairman) (1978) Special Educational Needs. London: H.M.S.O.

WEATHERLEY, R. and LIPSKY, M. (1977) Street level bureaucrats and institutional innovation: Implementing special education reform. Harvard Educational Review 47, 171-197

WELTON, J., WEDELL, K. and VARHAUS, G. (1982) Meeting Special Educational Needs: The 1981 Education Act and its Implications. London: University of London Institute of Education

WHITE, R. and BROCKINGTON, D. (1983) Tales Out of School. London: Routledge and Kegan Paul

WOLFENDALE, J. (1983) Parental Participation in Children's Development and Education. London: Gordon and Breach

References

WOODCOCK, M. and FRANCIS, D. (1981) Organisation Development
    Through Teambuilding. Farnborough: Gower
WOOLGAR, J. (1985) Piloting and Evaluating Parental Involve-
    ment with Children Experiencing Number Difficulties.
    Unpublished dissertation, M.Sc. Professional Training in
    Educational Psychology, North-East London Polytechnic

A.C.S.E.T.   28
action research   141-143, 147-148
appraisal   10, 12-18, 25, 47-49
attributions   19

behavioural anchors   16

careers officers   113, 119, 125
C.A.T.E.   28-29, 31
classroom assistants   132-133, 138-139
community care   7
conflict   20, 24, 93
consultancy   20-21, 23, 37, 72, 76,
                                82, 89, 96, 98, 104-110,
                                142
coordinators (special needs)   10, 74, 80, 83-88, 120,
                                123-126, 130-131
counselling   48, 49, 72, 74-75, 90,
                                117
C.P.V.E.   110, 120-121

deafness   5
doctors   18, 20, 119, 153
dyslexia   19, 130

Education Act 1970   29
Education Act 1976   28, 29
Education Act 1980   137

Subject Index

Education Act 1981   5, 35, 37, 43, 46, 57,
61, 67, 80, 81, 101, 120,
130, 137, 153, 156, 165,
169

educational psychologists   18, 19, 57, 62, 82, 87,
89, 90, 93, 94, 113, 119,
120, 127, 143, 153, 155,
158, 162

exchange theory   44

Fish Report   43, 67
Further Education   111-122

GRIST   18

hearing impairment   5, 57
H.M.I.   28, 29, 100
home tutors   126

I.N.S.E.T.- see staff development
interview   11, 17, 47, 49, 51, 117
interview style   55

job analysis   13-15, 18, 25
job descriptions   2, 12, 83-86, 132
job enrichment   45
job satisfaction   44, 91

management by objectives   14
medical officers   18, 82
motivation   7, 8, 115, 130, 149-150,
162-163, 169

negotiation   36, 44, 45, 54, 72,
79-80, 113, 121, 151
N.F.E.R.   40
nursery nurses   18

objectives   51, 105, 114, 116, 130,
                                   139

parents   23, 26, 40, 48, 49, 86,
                                   87, 112, 113, 119-120,
                                   126-128, 136-148, 163-164
pastoral care   89
personal constructs   150-151
physiotherapists   18, 20, 131
Plowden Report   136
Portage   137
psychiatric hospitals   7

resistance   55, 132, 140, 149
reward systems   56

scientific management   149
selection   10-13, 25, 87
self assessment   17, 155-170
selling services   95-98
SENIOS courses   10, 33, 35-42
social workers   7, 18, 20, 113, 119, 153,
                                   158
special schools   9, 71, 73, 76, 77, 79,
                                   86, 89, 112, 113
speech therapists   18, 20, 153
staff development   1, 16-18, 27-42, 43-65,
                                   73, 79, 81, 97, 101, 113,
                                   115, 116, 125
stress   21-25, 82, 116, 152
styles of intervention   106-107
support services   9-10,   38,   44,   66-81,
                                   82-98, 99-110, 123-126,
                                   128, 130-131, 134
systems approach   86, 140, 164-165

Taylor Report   137
teams   1, 88, 98, 103-104, 108,
                                   113, 115, 123-125, 140
tests   11, 87, 130, 144, 146,
                                   153, 154
time management   20, 94, 97
training - see staff development

Subject Index

T.V.E.I.   42, 110, 120-121

values   7-8, 56
visual impairment   114

Warnock Report   6, 28, 35, 43, 46, 62,
                                67, 71, 81, 82, 86, 101,
                                119, 120, 134, 137
whole-school approach   4, 9, 10, 70, 74, 75, 98,
                                99-110
withdrawal   71, 101